G000123409

"If you find yourself desp;
of our time, you will find

Alistair Begg explores the call of Jesus to a life that is radically different from what we see in the world and sometimes in the church: a life in which we love those with whom we radically disagree, speak with gentleness and kindness, and focus first on dealing with our own sins rather than the sins of others. This book is full of the grace and wisdom of Jesus, that we desperately need today."

COLIN SMITH, Senior Pastor, The Orchard Evangelical Free Church, Illinois; Founder, Open the Bible

"Alistair Begg brings the message of Jesus into our world, clarifying its meaning and relevance without blunting any of its challenge. But Begg also sets that challenge in the bigger context of Christ's message of grace. As a result, the challenge becomes an invitation—an invitation to a happy life."

TIM CHESTER, Crosslands Training; Author, *Enjoying God* and *Truth We Can Touch*

"Here is a book to be read slowly—and more than once. This is not because it is difficult to understand (it isn't), but because it is so important and good. Alistair Begg casts a brilliant light on the remarkable life into which Jesus calls his people. How does the life of a Christian actually show the reality of their salvation? How does it show their delight in values that are contrary to those of the world? Readers will find real answers. More than that, they will find themselves rejoicing in the privilege of being among those Jesus described as 'blessed.'"

JOHN WOODHOUSE, Retired Principal, Moore Theological College, Sydney, Australia

"Life in Jesus' kingdom is life at its very best—liberating, exhilarating, and altogether satisfying. It is also countercultural and counterintuitive. The principles and priorities of the kingdom are wildly different from the values and virtues celebrated in contemporary society, and it's all too easy for us to conform to the dominant culture rather than embrace our calling to live distinctively. With his typical blend of wisdom, warmth, and wit, Alistair Begg takes us back to Jesus' teaching and shows what kingdom life looks like—and why it really is the best life."

CAROLYN LACEY, Women's Worker, Woodgreen Evangelical Church, Worcester, UK; Author, *Say the Right Thing* and *Extraordinary Hospitality*

The
Christian
Manifesto

The
Christian
Manifesto

Alistair
Begg

The Christian Manifesto
© Alistair Begg, 2023

Published by:
The Good Book Company

thegoodbook.com | thegoodbook.co.uk
thegoodbook.com.au | thegoodbook.co.nz | thegoodbook.co.in

Published in association with the literary agency of Wolgemuth & Associates, Inc.

Cover design by Faceout Studio | Design and art direction by André Parker

ISBN Hardcover: 9781784989187 | JOB-007186   Printed in India
        Paperback: 9781784988708 | JOB-007182

Contents

An Invitation
to Happiness

How do you enjoy life at its very best?

Advertisers, of course, claim that they know the answer. Every commercial is seeking to make us feel discontent with how things are, in order to convince us that a better life will be found by buying what it's selling.

Politicians claim that they know the answer too. Every political address is asking us to trust that that person or party can put things right, and is trying to assure us that a better life will be found in voting for what they're offering.

At times, commercials and political speeches both point us back to a bygone era—the nostalgic impulse—when (if we squint, and forget the problems that existed at that time) everything was better: when our lives were purer or our hearts were lighter or our country was greater. At other times, they point us forward to the future and invite us to dream of how, if only we buy this or vote for that, all will soon be well.

So, amid the blizzard of offers and promises, to what or to whom are you looking to deliver life at its very best?

I want to take you to a description and a promise that you will never see in a commercial or hear from a politician. In this book, we're going to look at what can be helpfully seen as a "Christian manifesto." A manifesto is a public declaration or proclamation issued by a monarch or head of state, or by a representative of a company or organization. Here is a manifesto for the Christian life, straight from the lips of Jesus, as he gathered both his followers and those who were thinking about becoming his followers on "a level place"—on a plain—and taught them one of his most famous sermons, found in Luke's Gospel and known as the "Sermon on the Plain." It is a manifesto that is not oriented towards the political arena, but towards the relational and individual one.

At 725 words (in the ESV English translation), this manifesto is less than a third of the length of the average US presidential inaugural address. It is therefore, of course, not exhaustive—it does not cover every aspect of how Christ's people can live in a way that pleases him—but it is foundational. And in the first four words of his sermon, Jesus announces that what follows will be his answer to that question of where the best life is to be found:

"Blessed are you who…"

Kingdom Blessing

The word we translate "blessed" means "How happy!" "How fortunate!" or "How privileged!"[1] We all know people whom we look at and just think, "Your life is great. It's all fallen into place for you. You must be so happy. You

---

1 I owe this approach to the Sermon on the Plain, and the similar but longer Sermon on the Mount in Matthew's Gospel, to my friend John Woodhouse.

are so fortunate, so privileged." You're probably picturing someone right now. Those we consider blessed tend to be the wealthy or the successful or the powerful or the popular. Jesus looks at *his disciples*—his followers—and says that, even though they are none of those things, it is *they* who are blessed.

Why? Simply because they are members of his kingdom. The kingdom of God is one of the great themes of Luke: Luke records Jesus speaking of the kingdom of God (by my count) thirty times. The kingdom was what he *announced*: "I must," he told his disciples, "preach the good news of the kingdom of God to the other towns as well; *for I was sent for this purpose*" (Luke 4:43, emphasis mine). The kingdom was what he *revealed*, through his miracles; those who gathered to hear the Sermon on the Plain had come "to hear him and to be healed of their diseases" (6:18). These healings were a glimpse of what Jesus' eternal kingdom is like: a place where all that is wrong in this life is put right. The kingdom was what he *opened*, in his death and resurrection; the thief on the cross next to the Lord's, realizing who Jesus was and what he ruled, asked him to remember him "when you come into your kingdom" (23:42). It is an eternal kingdom, which will one day arrive in all its fullness but which for now exists in this world wherever its subjects are to be found (17:20-21).

And life in the kingdom of God was what Jesus *described* in the Sermon on the Plain: "Blessed are you who are poor," he began, "for yours is the kingdom of God." We shall return to this line in the next chapter, but Jesus is linking the life of true blessing with kingdom membership. Here is life as it is designed to be lived and enjoyed.

Here, as we shall see as Jesus continues to speak, is satisfaction, laughter, and joy—the full reality of what the advertisers and the politicians are offering us in their commercials and their manifestos.

An Invitation

The Sermon on the Plain, then, is Jesus' invitation to you to experience life at its very best. It is his description of what life in his kingdom—a kingdom where all that is wrong is being put right—looks like as we live in this world.

To be clear, the Lord is not describing how we *come into* the kingdom but how we *live in* the kingdom. As the great Reformer Martin Luther said of this passage, "Christ is saying nothing in this sermon about how we become Christians, but only about the works and fruit that no one can do unless he [or she] already is a Christian and in a state of grace."[2] These chapters, then, do not lay out a mechanism whereby someone becomes a Christian but the lifestyle of someone who is already a Christian. As Jesus told his disciples later in the Gospel of Luke, "Truly, I say to you, whoever does not receive the kingdom of God like a child shall not enter it" (Luke 18:17). A place in Jesus' eternal kingdom, with its satisfaction and laughter and joy, is something we receive from his hands, not something we have to gain or grasp with ours. Like children, we come to him and accept it as a gift, rather than bringing all we have done and achieved as a payment. But having come and received the kingdom from him, here, in this sermon, is an outline of what kingdom life today

2 *Luther's Works*, ed. Jaroslav Pelikan, vol. 21 (Concordia, 1958), p291.

is like. It is not exhaustive, but it is transformational. It shows us how kingdom membership transforms us from the inside out.

A Challenge

What we shall hear Jesus saying to us is radical—how faith in him compels and equips us to live out a new lifestyle that is often countercultural and counterintuitive. This makes the Sermon on the Plain not only an invitation but also a challenge. The hallmarks and priorities of Jesus' kingdom are different from this world's—and so its citizens will be different too. Jesus' call is deep, and it is wide, and it calls us to turn everything we naturally think upside down. Here we shall discover what the marks of a genuine Christian are. No one who is truly a member of Jesus' kingdom is left unchanged by that membership. Jesus says, *I want you to be happy about different things from what other people are happy about, and sad about things that other people don't routinely get sad about. I want you to have as your ambition something that the world regards as weak and ineffectual. I want you to treat people in a way that makes no sense to them and, at times, not much sense to you. I want you to have a different way of evaluating your decisions and your reactions and your life. I want you to be different.*

Jesus would not long have been employed by a 21st-century advertising agency, for he does not pretend that answering his call will be easy. He would not get far as a 21st-century politician either, for he does not flatter his hearers or compromise on his standards. But Jesus is neither an advertiser nor a politician; he was, and is, the eternal King, and he is not selling a product nor stumping for votes but announcing and describing his kingdom.

This is why I find this passage as hard as virtually any other. This manifesto is a description of the life we were all made for, but it is a challenge to be different from how I naturally am and how the world around me operates.

Make a Difference

This call to enjoy the blessing of life in Jesus' kingdom is, then, a call to be different. This is why it is the key to making a real difference in this world. Advertisers may make good money, and politicians may win fleeting power, but members of Jesus' kingdom can make a difference for eternity. For, to the extent that we are prepared to take seriously the standards and values of Jesus' kingdom and to display them as we live our lives, we will offer to the world around us an alternative and far better way to live than one that chases what the latest advert is selling or politician is offering. We will offer what John Stott referred to as "a Christian counterculture"[3]: a life that is harder and more uncomfortable and yet one that is truly satisfying and joyful and eternal.

The apostle Peter was one of those who was sitting and listening on that plain 2,000 years ago, as Jesus "lifted up his eyes on his disciples, and said, 'Blessed are you who…'" (Luke 6:20). Years later, Peter would describe members of Jesus' kingdom by reaching back to God's description of his Old Testament people:

---

3 *The Message of the Sermon on the Mount: Christian Counter-Culture* in The Bible Speaks Today series (IVP Academic, 1978).

> *"You are a chosen race, a royal priesthood, a holy*
> *nation, a people for [God's] own possession, that*
> *you may proclaim the excellencies of him who*
> *called you out of darkness into his marvelous light.*
> *Once you were not a people, but now you are God's*
> *people; once you had not received mercy, but now*
> *you have received mercy." (1 Peter 2:9-10)*

Peter is saying, *You need to know what you are—you're aliens and you're strangers; and so, as people who do not belong in this world, don't stop battling against everything, including your desires, that makes you want to live just like everyone else in this world. It's only as you live differently from this world that those around you (though they may fling accusations and derision at you) may actually come to see God's goodness through you, and give him glory when Jesus returns* (v 11-12, my paraphrase).

The best thing we have to offer those around us is the kingdom of Jesus, and the way to earn the right to speak to them about that kingdom is to show them that kingdom. The biggest reason for the ineffectiveness of contemporary Christianity is a failure to take seriously the radical difference that Jesus calls for as we follow him as King. The 21st-century Western evangelical church has too often given in to the temptation to soft-pedal Jesus' words—to find caveats and loopholes in what he says—in order to offer the world something that sounds more palatable and less demanding. We have spent decades congratulating ourselves for being able to go among our non-Christian friends and say, "You know what? We're just the same as you." And they've said, "You know what? I think you're absolutely right!" But if there is nothing different to be seen in the church, people will not see why they should consider listening to the church.

We are not called to be like the world, and the world does not need us to be like the world. We have something better to say because we have someone better to follow. That means the call of Christ to you and me is both greatly exciting and deeply challenging. The call is not to be comfortable but to be Christ-like—to discover the surprising means of experiencing real blessing, and in doing so to point others the way to it too.

In this book, then, as we listen to Jesus' Sermon on the Plain, we shall hear a manifesto describing what genuine Christianity looks like. It is upside down and right way up. It is surprising and wonderful. It is challenging and liberating. It is life at its very best—a blessed life, a kingdom life.

A Reversal
of Values

*"Blessed are you who are poor, for yours is the
kingdom of God." Luke 6:20*

Which would you rather be? You can choose one of
these two lists of four: poor, hungry, sad, and hated or rich, well fed, happy, and popular.

Jesus says that, though it sounds like a contradiction,
true happiness lies in turning our backs on all that promises to make us happy in this world:

> *"²⁰ And he lifted up his eyes on his disciples, and
> said:*
> *'Blessed are you who are poor, for yours is the
> kingdom of God.*
> *²¹ 'Blessed are you who are hungry now, for you
> shall be satisfied.*
> *'Blessed are you who weep now, for you shall laugh.*
> *²² 'Blessed are you when people hate you and when
> they exclude you and revile you and spurn your
> name as evil, on account of the Son of Man!*
> *²³ Rejoice in that day, and leap for joy, for behold,*

> *your reward is great in heaven; for so their fathers*
> *did to the prophets." (Luke 6:20-23)*

Jesus is describing a value system that is at total variance with that of the non-Christian world. We live in a contemporary setting that cries out for us to stand up for ourselves, be proud of ourselves, and elevate ourselves, and to be self-assertive in our pursuit of happiness. These values are what often lie behind our decisions to move house or chase promotions or retire early. This is often the impulse that directs the choice to get married and then to have kids; it's often why people choose to leave their marriages or neglect their kids. It's called being true to yourself, finding your truth, and living your best life, though in truth it's simply selfishness.

Jesus says that the route to true happiness is very, very different. He says that the path to it involves exalting what the world despises and rejecting what the world admires. "Blessed are you who are poor," he says, immediately countering some of the deepest assumptions of Western nations.

What does he mean?

The Problem With Wealth

Jesus is not saying that all poor people are saved, nor that no rich person is. If that were the case, an obviously prosperous businesswoman such as Lydia would never have had her eyes and her heart opened to the truth of the gospel (Acts 16:11-15). But what he is saying is that poverty yields a far greater response to the gospel than affluence, because poverty reminds us that we are dependent creatures and affluence lies to us that we are self-sufficient. This is why outward poverty may well be a means of spiritual blessing, because it leads a man or a woman to discover their utter dependence upon God—not only for physical and material things but also for spiritual blessings.

Have you noticed in the Gospels that rich people find it hard (not impossible, but very hard) to follow Jesus? Take the "rich young ruler" later in Luke's Gospel. He's a seeker, and he comes running up to Jesus, throws himself down on his knees, and says to him, "Good Teacher, what must I do to inherit eternal life?" (Luke 18:18). So far, so good. Yet two minutes later, he's walking away from Jesus, sad (v 23). Why? Because Jesus tells him to choose between his wealth and his Savior, and he chooses the wealth. Making that choice has actually made him feel worse, as well as meaning that he has turned his back on eternal life—but he cannot give his money up. Jesus uses the moment to teach his disciples a lesson about wealth: "How difficult it is for those who have wealth to enter the kingdom of God" (v 24). And then he employs a striking picture: "It is easier for a camel to go through the eye of a needle than for a rich person to enter the kingdom of God" (v 25).

Only if you think you could get a camel through the eye of a needle (and I can't even get the thread to go through) are you permitted to think that wealth is not a potential hazard when it comes to the Christian life. As Jesus challengingly puts it in the Sermon on the Plain, "Woe to you who are rich" (v 24). Jesus was teaching "a great crowd of his disciples and a great multitude of people" (v 17), and as he began to speak of the blessings of following him, he had "lifted up his eyes on his disc-iples" (v 20). Now, it seems to me, he was lifting his gaze from his immediate discipleship group and looking out on the crowd as he turned from the poor to the rich. He certainly wasn't addressing his disciples, because his disciples weren't rich. He was warning those who were interested in him but holding back from him, for one reason or another.

And he is cautioning them (and us) that putting wealth before him—allowing our hearts to be ruled more by accumulating more than worship of God—leads to "woe": misery, as the Phillips Bible translation paraphrases it. It is a very striking word—not a casual statement nor a statement of condemnation. Woe is the opposite of blessing. There is a sense of compassion in this word: "How terrible for you! How dreadful it is! How disappointing for you." Why are those who are rich facing woe? Because you who are rich "have received your consolation."

It is not that everyone who is rich has received their comfort from the world and can receive none from Christ. But Jesus is warning that if we are rich, we will find it hard not to look to our wealth for our comfort, to our money for solutions, and to our bank balance for security.

Who the Real Fool Is

It will be not be much further along in Luke's Gospel before Jesus describes the type of person whom God calls a "fool." Responding to a man who wants Jesus to intervene in his fight with his sibling over their inheritance, Jesus says, *I'm not going to pronounce on that. But I will warn you to look out: be on your guard against all covetousness, for one's life does not consist in the abundance of his possessions* (Luke 12:14-15). And to highlight the danger both this man and his brother are in, he tells them one of his famous parables, of a rich man who produced a good crop and basically said to himself, *I've got it made in the shade. I'll tear my barns down and build more, and then I'll say to myself, "You've got everything stored away, your bank account is in fantastic shape, and you can rest up and enjoy your golf; you've got plenty of good things laid up for many years. Take life easy; eat, drink and be merry."*

And God said to him, "Fool!"

Why? "This night your soul is required of you, and the things you have prepared, whose will they be?" (v 20).

"This," says Jesus, making clear the application for these squabbling brothers, "is how it will be with whoever stores up things for themselves..." (v 21, NIV)—but there is not a full stop there. If there were, then we would all need to make a vow of poverty and embrace a form of destitution. It does not just say, "This is how it will be with whoever stores up things for themselves," but "whoever who stores up things for themselves but is not rich toward God." *Woe to you,* Jesus says, *if you give the best of who you are to building wealth here and not to God; woe to you if you place your trust in your riches here and not in the eternal riches offered by God. Woe to you if you think that financial success and material prosperity is the key to your life, and so you fail to acknowledge your need of God; woe to you who are so rich in your own eyes that you refuse to run to God*—"for you have already received your comfort" (6:24, NIV). In other words, *You've had it.* It's like a small child who spends their allowance on nothing of any real value, and returns to ask their father for more, and hears the answer "You've had it."

Why is this a matter for misery? First, because if all we have is for this life, then we have nothing in the next one. That will be a matter of eternal regret. But second, because if all we have in this life is wealth, then in truth we have very little at all.

I remember years ago marrying a young couple. The husband was a stockbroker, and I asked him what had struck him in his work lately.

"Well, I opened my biggest account recently," he answered. "A man came in with his wife and deposited $30 million with me."

"And what struck you?" I asked.

"Well," he replied, "when he went to the restroom, his wife confided in me that their marriage was a shambles, that the money was a total nuisance to them, that they were purposeless in their existence, that they were held together by their wealth, and that their biggest concern was the arguments of their children over who was going to get what."

When all that a man or woman has is worldly wealth, they are poor indeed. What a tragedy. "Woe to you who are rich," says Jesus: *You've already had the reward, and it wasn't much.*

Imagine taking all the people who have ever lived and ranking them by wealth. If you are reading this in the West, it is very likely that you would be found in the top 1%. And therefore we need to hear the challenge of Jesus' words if we are to enjoy his promise, for wealth is what keeps so many people from following Christ wholeheartedly, and therefore from knowing the blessing of joyful dependence on our King. We're too rich. Too self-assured.

Too unwilling to admit to need or dependence. Too quick to explain what we've achieved and how we've done it. And therefore too unwilling to give up relying on ourselves in order to ask for help from the King; too unwilling to trust his commands rather than our insights.

The 16th-century pastor and theologian John Calvin put it like this: "He only who is reduced to nothing in himself and relies on the mercy of God is the one who is poor."[4] Christians are those who have bowed down and acknowledged our poverty of spirit and inability to gain what we most need. And so, having accepted that wealth is neither a god who will deliver satisfaction nor an indication that we can manage life with our own abilities and resources, we are freed to know the blessing of kingdom life. We can only enter the kingdom if we acknowledge our spiritual poverty—we can only enjoy the kingdom as we hold loose to any material plenty. "Godliness with contentment is great gain," Paul told Timothy, "for we brought nothing into the world, and we cannot take anything out of the world" (1 Timothy 6:6-7). Happier by far is the one who enjoys all things as a gift from God but does not forget their need of God.

The Trouble With Popularity
All of us want to be liked. In the West, most of us are unlikely to go hungry, but as Christians we are likely to be looked down upon. So it is striking that Jesus says that the life of blessing, the kingdom life, will involve being hated. "Blessed are you when people hate you" (Luke 6:22)—

---

4 *Commentary on a Harmony of the Evangelists, Matthew, Mark, and Luke,* trans. William Pringle, vol. 1 (The Calvin Translation Society, 1845), p261.

when you are excluded and insulted "on account of the Son of Man." Jesus is speaking of situations where it is our relationship with him that causes rejection or condemnation (not because we have been unkind or obnoxious or bitter). Sooner or later, if you hold the line for Jesus, you will discover that you are not liked.

You've likely experienced this. You've perhaps taken a stand for the truth and goodness of the Bible, or you've said, with faltering tongue, "Yes, I do believe that Jesus is the person that he claimed to be, the only Savior, the only way to be right with God." And all of a sudden you found yourself isolated and a little removed from your peer group—or worse. It may happen in your office or your school or your neighborhood. Our natural response is to pursue a policy of appeasement, by never saying anything that might offend. The Christian way is to pursue a policy of truth, seeking to say what most needs to be said: that Jesus is Lord and that he offers to save anyone who comes to him, but that we must come to him; that "there is salvation in no one else, for there is no other name under heaven given among men by which we must be saved" (Acts 4:12). That was the message of the first disciples, who were more reviled than we are likely to be and yet who were more full of joy than we seem to be. When we are hated for saying what is true, we should regard it as a cause for joy. After all, being treated like this is a sign that we truly are members of the kingdom of Christ—and it is being in his kingdom that gives us life, now and for eternity. Being mocked for our faith will not remove our blessing if our sense of joy did not come from our reputation in the first place.

On the other hand, being governed by how well-liked we are is a path to "woe"; "Woe to you, when all people speak well of you," warns Jesus. Again, this is countercultural. But, as Jesus points out, it has always been "false prophets" rather than truth-tellers who have found popularity. It is virtually impossible to have everybody speak well of us unless we speak out of both sides of our mouths, saying one thing to one person and another thing to another, and always only saying what people want to hear. That is what the false prophets did, preaching peace when invasion was coming, assuring people that their lives were in good order when in truth God was angry with their injustice and hypocrisy. If we want everybody to speak well of us, we will have to sacrifice our principles left, right, and center. It is a miserable thing, Jesus says, to lose the truth and to lose yourself in order to be liked.

Christians Cry

In between his warnings of woe to those who chase wealth or reputation are two more. The first is a warning aimed at "you who are full now."

Woe to you, in other words, *who are laboring under the delusion that you have no need of God—because one day you're going to go hungry.* Here's the individual who knows everyone and is liked by everyone: who is never short of friends, who is always invited to everything, and who always seems to have been given tickets to every event and can skip the line when they get there. They seem to have it all together. They themselves are sure that they do have it all together.

Most of us want, deep down, to be that kind of person. Our society is driven by these things. But if that's all a person has, they are about to become incredibly hungry. Successful people are often self-sufficient people, and self-sufficient people tend to be self-satisfied. If their lives never take a turn for the worse—if they are never "hungry"—they will never discover their need of someone beyond themselves. They will live with the illusion that they have no need of anyone to supply anything to them. They will discover too late that they too have lived as fools, for one day their life will be taken from them, and there will remain only an insatiable hunger that will last for all of eternity. Can you imagine wanting a drink of water forever? Can you imagine feeling empty because of a hunger that never stops? Can you imagine being lonely with a loneliness that can never be assuaged?

Jesus is speaking about the ultimate realities of life—including eternal life. The way to be truly happy now is to live in light of his divinity and our eternity, he is saying. We will only truly enjoy life now if we have settled the issue of what life will be then; the way to learn to live is to settle the issue of how to die and what lies beyond. And so "blessed are you who are hungry now"—who are hungering for more than this world offers or than you can supply for yourself—"for you shall be satisfied." Blessed is the person who has not settled for the pleasures of this life, who is not blind to the frustrations of this life, and who therefore hungers for more.

This leads on to Jesus' other woe-warning—against a kind of flippant approach that laughs its way through life: "Woe to you who laugh now, for you shall mourn and weep." Again, Jesus is not saying that his people are those who never laugh. Laughter is a gift from God—in fact, it is the right response to the enormity and wonder of his blessings (see Genesis 21:6; Psalm 126:2). What Jesus is referring to here is the laughter of fools: the approach that makes everything funny, rendering nothing truly worth laughing about—the mindset of the person who refuses to contend with reality because they are determined always to find levity. But life in this fallen world involves tragedy as well as comedy, and the person who insists only on laughter is the person who cannot feel for others or comfort others and who has no reserves to fall back on when their own circumstances take the smile from their face. That's why the wise man in Ecclesiastes says, "It is better to go to the house of mourning than to go to the house of feasting ... The heart of the wise is in the house of mourning, but the heart of fools is in the house of mirth" (Ecclesiastes 7:2, 4). It is in tragedy that there is a greater opportunity for us to face the reality of life.

"Blessed are you who weep now," says Jesus. Blessing comes to the person whose view of this world is robust enough to be able to take account of the reality that life includes funerals as well as parties, and who is willing to weep for and with the suffering. For only those who have reckoned with the darkness of life, and only those who know that one day the darkness shall pass, can truly appreciate the moments of joy, as they look forward to the coming of the kingdom in all its fullness, when God shall wipe every tear from our eyes. And so it is those who are willing to weep now who "shall [then] laugh" (Luke 6:21).

Which Would You Rather?

So here we have it: blessing promised for those who are poor, hungry, weeping, and hated; misery pronounced upon those who are rich, full, flippant, and popular. The characteristics of Christian discipleship are, from the world's perspective, the marks of losers. And characteristic of the ungodly are those who have made it. The Lord Jesus is here proclaiming woe to the American dream—and the dream of every wealthy Western 21st-century society.

It's so difficult for us to apply what Jesus is saying to us here because, frankly, we are surrounded by so much. But the Christian is called to be different. You can sign up anywhere for a life of wealth, plenty, flippancy, and popularity. The only cost is misery and an eternity without Jesus. But there is only one place where you can sign up for the happiness of life with Jesus now and forever—for a life that is poor, hungry, sad, hated... and blessed. That place is the cross—the place where the Lord himself gave up everything, was thirsty, cried out in anguish, was mocked... and yet endured it all for our good and for the joy that was set before him (Hebrews 12:2). That is the challenge—to acknowledge your dependence and poverty and need, and come to him. There we discover the power to live our lives upside down in the eyes of this world and right way up in the eyes of our Savior.

The genuine Christian is poor, hungry, crying, and hated—and they have found blessing, for with these things come satisfaction and joy. These are the marks of life in the kingdom of God. Which would you rather be? Poor, hungry, crying, and hated or rich, well fed, flippant, and popular? True happiness does not lie in the obvious and natural choice but in the countercultural and Christian one.

An Exceptional
Kind of Love

"Love your enemies." Luke 6:27

The Christian shows in their life that their salvation is a reality. The true Christian points not to a baptismal certificate or a decision made years ago but to their life in the present as evidence that their faith is real. And here is the next simple yet deeply challenging mark of the Christian. Jesus lays it out in these three simple words: "Love your enemies."

Imagine someone standing in the crowd, saying to their friend, "Did Jesus just say what I think he did? Did Jesus just say you're supposed to actually love your enemies?" And their friend says, "Shh, wait a minute. You're missing the rest of it!" And so they bend their ears toward Jesus in time to hear him say, "Do good to those who hate you, bless those who curse you, pray for those who abuse you."

Jesus is teaching that his followers are not simply to do what is right but what is good. And they are to act in this way not only towards those who deserve it but towards those who don't. Why? Because "your Father is merciful" (v 36). It is incongruous, if not impossible, for those of us who declare ourselves to be the children of our heavenly Father not to manifest the mercy of our merciful God and not to display a love for our enemies—incongruous for those of us who profess to be followers of Jesus not to approach those who wrong us in the way that he did, who, "when he was reviled ... did not revile in return ... but continued entrusting himself to him who judges justly" (1 Peter 2:23).

The issue here, then, is simply this: love. Everyone has something to say about love—poets, song writers, celebrities. I fairly regularly hear someone say something like "Well, all you need is love, as the good book says." Setting aside the fact that it was Lennon and McCartney, not God, who said, "All you need is love," there's a sense in which it's true: we certainly need love more than we need hate, and we can all see what hate is doing to our world and perhaps even in our own communities or families.

But it's one thing to sing it; it's another thing to understand what love is, and it is still another to actually put into practice the command to love.

Love Is...

So, what is love? The word that we find in the New Testament for "love" is a translation of one of three Greek words for "love" used in the New Testament, and there are actually four Greek words for "love" that are translated by our one English word.

First, *storge,* which is the Greek word for "natural affection." It's the kind of affection that should exist between two sisters in a family. There is a natural dimension to it. They love each other; it is a *storge* kind of love. Second, *eros*, which is a romantic or sensual love. Third, *philia* or *phileo*, which is the word that provides part of the name of Philadelphia, "The City of Brotherly Love." This doesn't have to do with the natural affection of people within the same family but with a sense of brotherliness and camaraderie such as members of a sports team or an exercise club may have together.

None of those words is the one used by Jesus here, though. Here, the word is *agape*. And this is radically different because this is a love which is not drawn out by the identity or attractiveness or merit of the one who is being loved. It's not that we look at them and think, "Oh, this is a lovely person. Naturally, I feel a level of affection towards them." Jesus is calling for a love for people that is in no way related to their lovability.

Agape is, of course, the kind of love that God has for you in Christ. He does not love you because you've cleaned up your act, or because you're spiritually attractive, or because your works merit his affection. No, we "were by nature children of wrath," for we were "dead in the trespasses and sins in which [we] once walked" (Ephesians 2:3, 1). "But God shows his love for us in that while we were still sinners, Christ died for us … *while we were enemies* we were reconciled to God by the death of his Son" (Romans 5:8, 10, emphasis added).

If these are familiar verses to you, do not let them wash over you. Savor them. It is only because God chooses to love those who live as his enemies that you have any hope, any relationship with him, and anything to look forward to in eternity. God loves his enemies—and his children, Jesus says, are to do the same.

Agape love is not blind. Jesus is not saying we exercise this kind of love for our enemies by being blind to their offenses against us or because somehow love takes over and we don't see people as they really are. He's saying that we see them exactly as they are—in all of their ugliness, their spitefulness, their cursing, their hatred, their unwillingness to pay us what they owe us—in all that would naturally cause us to see them as adversaries. *See all of that person's flaws and wrongs clearly and plainly,* says Jesus. *And then love them.*

The Bible scholar Richard Lenski puts it like this:

> *"This love may see nothing attractive in the one loved. Nor is this love called out by anything that is attractive. Its inner motive, be the object worthy or not, is to bestow these blessings upon the one loved and to do him the highest possible good."* [5]

Jesus is, once again, taking conventional human wisdom and turning it completely on its head. The standard approach is this: you like people you're supposed to like, and you hate people you're allowed to hate. If people treat you well, if your affections are drawn out by who they are or how they are, then love them well; if people treat you badly, then at best you are called to tolerate them, and in most circumstances it's entirely justifiable to get even with them. Jesus says, "Do good to those who hate you." That's the opposite from what our hearts want to do and what our world tells us to do.

As an aside, Jesus is not here correcting Old Testament teaching but rather continuing it. There is a common

---

5 *The Interpretation of St. Luke's Gospel 1–11* (Augsburg Fortress, 2008), p 361 (paraphrased).

misconception that the Old Testament said, *Love your neighbor; hate your enemy.* It did not. Leviticus 19:18 says to God's people, "You shall not take vengeance or bear a grudge against the sons of your own people, but you shall love your neighbor as yourself. I am the LORD."

How does anyone get to *Hate your enemies; love your neighbors* from that? Simple: they take the little phrase "your own people" and use it to shrink and diminish the notion of comprehensive love. They determine who "your own people" are and define them as those who are easy to love. Think like this and you can conclude that you are excused from having to love anyone who crosses you or is not much like you. And so Jesus says, in effect, *Read Leviticus 19:18. Who are your people? Everyone. Who is your neighbor? Everyone.*

Therefore, *Do not bear a grudge* applies to your relationship with everyone whom you could bear a grudge against—that is, everyone who has wronged you. That will challenge almost all of us. Some of us have grudges that don't just go back months; they go back years. And we carry them around. We nurture them as if they were comfortable little toys. We bring them out to the forefront of our minds from time to time and re-examine them. We may never act on them, but we imagine how satisfying it would be to do so.

"Love your enemies," says our Lord. "Do good to those who hate you."

Love Is Action
So, what does this look like? Jesus gives us some specific examples:

- If someone hits you, offer him your other cheek, not your fist.
- If someone takes something from you, be generous to them.
- If someone asks for something from you, give it.
- If someone borrows something and does not return it, make it a gift.

We need to be careful here. We are called to take Jesus' words literally—that is, to take the literal sense and meaning and application—but not literalistically—so that if someone hits you, you ask them to hit you on the other side of your face. Jesus himself did not do that; when, in John 18, he was struck by one of the temple officials, he did not turn around in order to be struck again, but instead he protested the injustice.

Jesus is not calling his followers to some weak form of passivity which enables evil. He never told us not to restrain the murderer's hand, not to stand up against the abuser, not to check the thief, not to oppose dishonesty. What, then, is the principle that Jesus is making concrete here? It's simply this: that when we receive an injury, we must not seek revenge. Indeed, we must be ready to take another injury if necessary because it is more than likely that the person will come back and have another go at us.

Put another way, we are not to be normal. "Normal" is to respond with like for like—to meet force with force, and insult with insult, and malice with malice. "Normal" is to deprive others of your blessing if they treat you wrongly. What is Christian is to seek to do what's best for your enemy in the same way as you would for your spouse or your best friend.

This is radically countercultural. It always has been. First-century Roman society was based on patronage—a benefactor raised up those who came to him or her for help, and then they owed them their allegiance and love. If someone gave to you, you were in their debt, and so you gave back to them. If someone helped you, you were honor-bound to help them. Jesus is saying, *Those are not the principles you are to live by. This is what I want you to do: I want you to form a community that is marked by a refusal to treat others according to what they deserve or what they can do for you. Even those who hate, exclude, revile, and defame you are not to be treated as enemies. I want you to live in a community marked by a refusal to treat others as though they were your enemies.* This attitude is to be—*has* to be—revealed through actions. And these actions are to be positive and proactive. Jesus is not talking about doing no one any harm; he is talking about doing everyone actual good. It's not enough to refrain from hostility. Our deeds and our words are to display the love of Christ.

The Family Likeness

If we view what Jesus is saying here only in terms of a prescription for moral behavior, we miss the point. Jesus is not wanting you to read his words, finish this chapter, close up the book, and think, "Right. I am supposed to love my enemies. I will go and get on with that." And you'll be driving and someone will cut in front of you and then curse at you, and you will remember Jesus' words, refrain from making an ugly sign back, and pray, "Lord, bless that lovely sinner over there in that blue Ford pickup truck." If he goes as far as shouting out the window to suggest to you that you are a very bad person and to question your parentage, then you will not reply in kind and you'll smile at him instead of telling him what you would like to tell him. And you'll grit your teeth, and you'll do the "love your enemies" thing.

What is the problem here? It is that in doing this, you will be purporting to love your neighbor, but you will not be loving God. You will just be doing what you have to do so that you can check off Luke 6:27 and feel better about yourself. Here is how that will go: it will lead to pride, and it will also lead to an unconscious desire to find some loopholes in the command so that you can tell yourself you're keeping it and feel good that you are keeping it at the least possible cost to yourself. Sooner or later, you will find yourself watering down what "love" and "do good" and "bless" mean, and you will limit who the people are whom you are called to treat well. Before too long, in your thinking, that guy in the blue pickup won't count as your neighbor, and cursing at him will seem reasonable and justifiable.

So what is the *right* way to take this command, if it is not simply to go and get on with obeying it?! It is to first remember that this is how God chose to treat you, for "your Father is merciful" (v 36). It was "while we were enemies [that] we were reconciled to God by the death of his Son" (Romans 5:10). It is to believe that Jesus has the right to tell you what is right and best. It is to reflect on God's mercy to you so that you are renewed and transformed in your mind (Romans 12:1-2), so that you want to love others because you love the God who so loves you. It is to appreciate that to live this way is to bear the family likeness, to be "merciful … as your Father is merciful." When we approach the command like this, we do not balk at its clarity and seek to find opt-outs in its application. We no longer seek to obey it minimally but wholeheartedly—we do not do what we must but all we can.

What Does the World See?

Here is the challenge and the opportunity: would the average non-Christian look at the evangelical church as embodying this principle? Or is it distinctly possible that people have been left with the impression that conservative Christianity takes the approach that only if you agree with our doctrines, and often with our politics, do you get to experience our kindness and love—and if you do not, then you will be disregarded and demonized? Do you think the average student on a university campus or family in your community would read "Love your enemies" and think of evangelical Christians as exemplifying this command or as setting it aside?

There is a reason that when Jesus told his famous Parable of the Good Samaritan a little further on in Luke's Gospel (Luke 10), he chose to identify the two men who walked past the injured man on the roadside as religious leaders, and also chose to make the hero who stopped to care for the bleeding man the least likely character—a member of the hated Samaritan nation. Jesus told that parable to answer a legal expert who, trying to limit what love looks like, asked, "Who is my neighbor?" The question, Jesus says in response, is "Which of these three [men who came across the bleeding man] proved to be a neighbor" to him (Luke 10:36)? And the lawyer, who by now was presumably wishing he had never begun this conversation, replies, "The one who showed him mercy" (v 37). *Exactly,* says Jesus. *So go and live like that. Your neighbor is whoever you come across, and you are to love them regardless of who they are or what they have done for you or to you.*

There is no one you are not called to love, for "your Father is merciful" to his enemies. The love of which Jesus speaks here redefines the boundaries. The follower of Jesus does not get to pick whom he or she loves. There is no inner circle. The distinctions and barriers are all dismantled by Jesus' words here.

It will only be when the church is prepared to live this out—when we resemble the good Samaritan more than the two religious leaders—that we will make an impact on our countries and their cultures. Championing a political cause and pursuing a political fix is simply not what Jesus primarily called his people to do. Loving our enemies is. We will only make a positive difference when people say, "I stand for everything they disagree with. I have treated them without kindness. And yet they have responded with respect, and they have done their best to be good to me, and they have not merely tolerated me but they have loved me. I don't agree with their take on this issue or that question—but I cannot deny that there is a love there that I cannot explain."

I'll show you how to make an impact on the culture, says Jesus. *Love your enemies, do good to those who hate you, bless those who curse you, and pray for those who ill-treat you.* If we chose to live this out, it would cause a revolution in our culture. It would prompt a complete change in the tone that many of us adopt on social media. It would open doors of homes and make them places of welcome and restoration. It would cause bridges to be built across political divides that have caused disagreements (or worse) in the past, and it would transform relationships in the workplace into ones of collaboration and forgiveness rather than self-promotion and grudge-holding. In other words, if we chose to live this out, it would show what our Father is like: merciful. It would show that there is a different way to live: that this life is not all there is, that these possessions are not all we have, and that getting what we can and keeping what we want is not the only way to operate. "Love your enemies," says Jesus. If that doesn't challenge you, you have not understood what he is saying to you. If it does challenge you, then do not close this book without dropping to your knees and praying to your merciful Father, asking...

> *May the mind of Christ my Savior dwell in me from day to day,*
> *By His love and power controlling all I do and say.*
> *May the love of Jesus fill me as the waters fill the sea;*
> *Him exalting, self-abasing, this is victory.*[6]

"Him-exalting, self-abasing, this is victory"—what a wonderful inversion of the way this world orders itself. "Love your enemies, do good to those who hate you."

6 Kate B. Wilkinson (1925).

What the Golden Rule
Really Means

*"As you wish that others would do to you,
do so to them." Luke 6:31*

Here is perhaps the most frequently misquoted verse in the Bible (though it has a close rival, which we will come to in the next chapter). It is what is often referred to as the "Golden Rule," and it's one of a handful of verses that still, in our increasingly post-Christian Western societies, is well-known to the average person. It is a statement that has been hijacked by all kinds of people and pressed into service in all kinds of ways, often without any real understanding or consideration of its context or its meaning. So, we need to hit pause and take some time to ask: what did Jesus actually mean?

The Rule

As we saw in the previous chapter, Jesus makes it clear that members of his kingdom—those who are children of God—are to love others. Prior to the time of Jesus, this rule had been pronounced only in a negative form. As we saw in the previous chapter, Leviticus 19:18 told God's people, "You shall not take vengeance or bear a grudge against the sons of your own people, but you shall love your neighbor as yourself." In the 1st century BC, in the writings of the influential Jewish rabbi Hillel, this was interpreted thus: "What is hateful to you, do not do to your neighbor." Jesus, on the other hand, states it positively. He is making it clear that it is not simply enough for his followers to be passive, to refrain from recrimination or revenge; no, the children of God are to be initiative-takers in this matter of love.

This Golden Rule is not uniquely found in the Bible. In one form or another, it appears all over the place. You can find it in the writings of the ancient Greek writers: of Plato, of Aristotle, and of Seneca. You can find it in the writings of the Chinese philosopher Confucius too. But in every other instance, it comes without the framework which is essential if we are to be able first to understand it and then to apply it properly.

The first key to understanding the Bible's teaching on the Golden Rule is that the way to keep it is to obey God's law. In Romans 13, Paul says:

> "The commandments, 'You shall not commit
> adultery, You shall not murder, You shall not steal,
> You shall not covet,' and any other commandment,
> are summed up in this word: 'You shall love your
> neighbor as yourself.' Love does no wrong to a
> neighbor; therefore love is the fulfilling of the law."
> (v 9-10)

So God's laws are summed up in the Golden Rule; but God's laws also describe how to keep the Golden Rule. If you want to love your neighbor, do not kill them or sleep with their spouse (obviously!). If you want to love your neighbor, obey God's laws in the way you treat them. You love others by obeying God; and loving others can never look like disobeying God.

The law, rather than our own wisdom or our neighbors' preferences, is the standard that defines what love looks like. As the apostle John puts it, "I ask you [to] love one another. And this is love, that we walk according to his commandments; this is the commandment, just as you have heard from the beginning, so that you should walk in it" (2 John v 5-6). To return to Romans 13, it's striking that Paul tells his readers to love their neighbor by obeying God's word and then continues, "you know the time, that the hour has come for you to wake from sleep. For salvation is nearer to us now than when we first believed" (v 11). Paul is saying that, having taught these Roman Christians the foundational elements of Christianity, he is moving from the doctrinal indicatives (who we are in Christ) to the moral imperatives (how we live for Christ). And the summary of these is to love your neighbor as yourself by obeying God's commands in how you treat them.

Second, we cannot separate the command to love people from the commandment to love God. Fairly commonly you will hear someone—a politician espousing a particular policy or a friend trying to find common ground between religions, or even a church leader seeking to sound palatable in the secular media—sum up the teaching of Jesus as "Love your neighbor. Do to others as you would have them do to you." Did Jesus say that? Yes. Did Jesus say that only that? No—and he never told us to love our neighbor as ourselves without also telling us to love God with all that we have. He never separated love for God from love for others. "Which is the greatest commandment of all?" a religious expert asked him. What did Jesus answer?

> "The most important is, 'Hear, O Israel: The Lord
> our God, the Lord is one. And you shall love
> the Lord you God with all your heart and with
> all your soul and with all your mind and with
> all your strength.' The second is this: 'You shall
> love your neighbor as yourself.' There is no other
> commandment greater than these."
>
> (Mark 12:28-31)

Jesus did not say, *The summation of the law is this: love your neighbor as yourself.* No—he said, *Love the one true God with everything you have, and one way you do so is to love your neighbor as yourself.*

Those around us are very happy with the idea of loving others as we would like to be loved ourselves. No one is going to reject that! Where they part ways with the Christian is at "The Lord is one"—at the idea that he will accept no rivals, for he has no rivals—and therefore that we are to love God as God in every way, in every moment.

Third, we are not to look to our own strength to keep this rule. People customarily believe that they can actually live this out. They hear "Love your neighbor as yourself" and "Do to others as you would have them do to you," and they say to themselves, "That is excellent, and very straightforward. Now I'm going to go out and have a very good try at that." Religious people are doing this all the time: "This is how to live, so I will go and live that way." It is simple, and it is impossible. Let me tell you: you cannot do it.

Left to ourselves, we may be able to see how we should live; but, by ourselves, we will sooner or later discover that it is a way that we are unable to live. That's why religion as an external code of practice presented to well-meaning people Sunday after Sunday is the most dreadful tyranny. When the pastor says, "Now go out and love your enemies" and the people think, "Right, I will go out and do that," if they are sufficiently self-aware, at some point during the week (very possibly within hours of leaving church) they will realize, "I did not treat that person well. Even those closest to me, whom I love so much—I don't treat them well." They have a miserable week. And they come back and say, "You know, I need to try harder" and eventually they don't come back because they've said, "I can't do this. I give up."

What lies at the root of this? It is this: that religious people think that by obeying God, they will make themselves his children. The truth is the absolute reverse: Christians understand that, having been made God's children by grace, they seek to obey him, and that it is only because they have God working in them that they are they able to do what God calls for in their lives. As Paul says in Philippians 2:12-13, we are to "work out your own salvation with fear and trembling, for it is God [who works within] you both to will and to work for his good pleasure." It is only as God works in you that you are able to do what God calls for from you. You can make an attempt at it on your own, but you cannot achieve it

47

because what Jesus calls for here is not the natural response of natural men and women but the supernatural response of kingdom subjects.

The Question

Once we understand what the Golden Rule actually is, we are ready to listen to Jesus teach us about what it will look like practically:

> *"If you love those who love you, what benefit is that to you? For even sinners love those who love them. And if you do good to those who do good to you, what benefit is that to you? For even sinners do the same. And if you lend to those from whom you expect to receive, what credit is that to you? Even sinners lend to sinners, to get back the same amount." (Luke 6:32-34)*

Jesus asked essentially the same question three times: what benefit or credit do we deserve for loving those who love us back—for doing things for those who can do something for us? If we do good to those who do good to us—well, that is just what everyone else does. That is not what God is calling us to. Loving someone who loves you does not mean you get to drive around with a bumper sticker that says, "I am an honors graduate in the school of love."

Again, Jesus is calling us to a radical lifestyle that is dramatically different from the framework of the surrounding culture, both in his day and in ours. You don't get points for acting in reciprocity. After all, a "you scratch my back, and I'll scratch yours" approach is one that "even sinners" live up to. Jesus uses this little two-word phrase deliberately because the religious people of his day would have spat out that phrase. Religious people, then and now, are glad that they're not as bad as others. Central to a religious approach to life is that there are better people—including you—and worse people—sinners. Later in Luke's Gospel, and not long before he meets the rich young ruler, Jesus will tell a parable that is in many ways a summary of the whole gospel—the story of the Pharisee and the tax collector (Luke 18:9-14). The religious leader says, "God, I thank you that I am not like other men." That is his big claim to approval: *I'm doing better. I'm obeying you, I'm doing the religious things, I'm checking the boxes, my tithing is sorted and I'm fasting twice as much as anyone would expect. I am not like that tax collector over there. I am glad that I'm not like him.*

Jesus juxtaposes that attitude with the one of the tax collector, who has a very different view of himself: "God, be merciful to me, a sinner!" The disciples are implicitly being posed a question:

Q: Which of the two was justified—that is, accepted by God?

A: It's not the religious guy.

That's why Jesus uses the words "even sinners" as he talks about what it looks like to truly love your neighbor as yourself. If you like to think of yourself as a religious person, a good person, a not-particularly-sinful person… well, ok, but are you basically loving only those who love you, doing good only to those who are doing good to you, and lending only to those who can pay back? Because if that's you, you're no better than the people you are proud that you're better than. You're not better than them at all! Whoever it is that you naturally look down upon—you're just like that.

So, think about who you are kind to. Think about who you invite over to your home. Think about those for whom you go out of your way. If it's only those from whom you get something, then none of that marks you out as a follower of Christ, the one who loved us before we ever loved or did anything for him (Romans 5:8; 1 John 4:19). None of that draws praise from Christ. It's just what everyone else is doing, one way or another.

The Action

The proof that we understand how we have been loved by God, says Jesus, is love for our enemies. Remember, this kind of love is possible only because God enables us, through his Spirit, to live this way. God calls us to do the impossible and then empowers us to do it.

Loving your neighbor as yourself, when the category of neighbor includes everyone you meet, including your enemies, is a supernatural action, and it is an action that is the proof of our salvation.

Do not miss the challenge of this. Jesus is saying, *Are you mine?* For your answer, don't point to your baptism but to your love for those who can't give much back. Here's the deal: Jesus is saying that we prove ourselves to be the sons of the Most High—not exclusively, not solely, but primarily—in the way we love and do good and are generous to our enemies, without expectation of anything in return. This is supposed to be an uncomfortable challenge. It is certainly very uncomfortable to me.

Here is how I think through what it would mean for me to live out Jesus' command myself. I think of people who are behaving in a way that rejects God and his ways, that undermines what God says glues societies and families together, and who do it publicly while mocking Christians as bigots. Naturally, I do not like them. But I am called to the supernatural work of loving them. Not ignoring them, not avoiding them, but actively seeking to bless them. I am not called to walk on past them, like the religious leaders in the Parable of the Good Samaritan; no, I'm called to be like the Samaritan, who is the classic illustration of loving and lending and doing good without a calculator, without the expectation of a payback—who said (in the wonderful words of the King James Version) to the innkeeper he took the injured man to, "And whatsoever thou spendest more, when I come again, I will repay thee" (Luke 10:35). Jesus is saying, *That, Alistair, is the attitude I want you to take and the actions I want you to take most of all toward the people whom you feel like treating that way least of all.*

The Reward
What happens as we take on this challenge—as we prayerfully head out into the world seeking to do unto others as we would have them do to us?

> *"Your reward will be great, and you will be sons of the Most High, for he is kind to the ungrateful and the evil." (Luke 6:36)*

This is not saying that as a result of doing these things, you will become the son or daughter of the Most High God. (It is "the ungrateful and the evil" who God is kind to, without regard for their moral goodness.) No, Jesus is saying that as a result of doing these things, you will reveal yourself to be a child of God. You will "be merciful, even as your Father is merciful" (v 37). And that is the reward, I think. People will look at you and say, in effect, "You are so very like your Father." Do you know what it means to a child who admires their father when they are compared to him? It makes them stand a little taller. It makes them walk a little more joyfully. They think to themselves, "Well, I don't see much of my father in myself, to be honest. I wouldn't have made that comparison. But that person said I'm like my father, so to some extent I must be."

Not only that, but we can know that when we love others regardless of their loveliness, God himself is looking at us and saying, in effect, *They are acting in the way that I act. They are like me in that.* Do you know what it means to a child who admires their father for *their own father* to say, "Well done. I'm pleased with you"?

That's what Jesus says: *By your loving, by your lending, by your doing good, you so begin to look like your Father.* God has showered his love upon his people—it is not a trickle, it is a torrent—and as our hearts are filled with our Father's love, so out of our hearts may flow his love toward others. And as we live this way, this is the greatest reward, the most wonderful blessing: we get to show we are his, to know we are his, and to know that we are becoming like him.

Do Something
Again, if we really treat others in the way we would like to be treated—if we really treat others in the way our Father

treats us—then we will be showing a supernatural love to a world that operates very differently. This means we need to beware of creating little holy huddles, taking care of each other and spending our time with one another in a closed shop called evangelical Christianity. Of course it is not wrong to help each other out; but it is wrong to do so exclusively, at the expense of helping out those who are our enemies.

Jesus' words, then, call us to an uncomfortable approach to life that is utterly different to the one our culture and our own instincts recommends to us, for it seeks proactively and positively to love those who give nothing back. I do not know what obeying Jesus' command here needs to look like for you, in your specific circumstances, but I do know that it needs to look like *something*—something tangible, something practical. It does not look like cheering from the sidelines or advocating for political change while not being prepared to actually do something.

If I think that by supporting a welfare package, I've done for others what Jesus calls for, I am wrong, unless I am prepared simultaneously to mentor the children of poverty and draw alongside the boys and the girls who live without fathers.

If I think that by criticizing and arguing against the gay-rights lobby or the trans-rights lobby, I have done what Jesus calls for, I am wrong, unless I am also prepared to bring some measure of kindness and hope to those who are living that lifestyle or in that identity and finding it not to deliver what they had been promised it would, or who are suffering with AIDS or regretting undergoing irreversible surgery.

If I think that by advocating for or applauding the over-turn of Roe v. Wade, I am doing for others what Jesus calls for, I am wrong, unless I am at the same time prepared to open my heart, my home, and my checkbook to show vulnerable and scared women the radical difference that Jesus makes.

There's a reason that C.H. Spurgeon did not only preach evangelistically but was involved in orphanages. There's a reason that D.L. Moody not only aimed to make an impact by proclaiming the gospel but by building schools and founding a publishing house. In previous generations, churches built hospitals and orphanages and libraries. In ours, we build atriums, gyms, and coffee houses. Our society is not suffering from a surfeit of Christians who have read their Bibles and said to themselves, "I'm going to shower with love the people who do not share my faith or my ethics or my approach. I'm going to show people what it means to be loved without having to give anything back." But imagine if it were. Imagine if you said that, and, by the Spirit's power, lived that. What a difference that would make.

Generous

Forgiveness

"Judge not, and you will not be judged ... forgive,
and you will be forgiven." Luke 6:37

The rich man's beautiful wife was upstairs getting ready for bed, and their baby was asleep in the nursery when his friend appeared at the front door. It seemed an idyllic scene: except for the fact that the woman should never have been this man's wife. She was only there because he had allowed lust to lead to immorality, which had led to her falling pregnant. He had covered things up as best he could, by organizing the removal of her husband and taking her as his wife. And that was all in the past now, and he was banking on everything increasingly feeling like water under the bridge.

Then his friend turned up.

The rich man welcomed him in, and they sat down together. "I have a story I want to tell you," the visitor said to his host. "It's a story about two men who both lived in a certain town."

"Go on," said the man.

"Well," he said, "one was rich and had plenty of sheep and cattle. The other man had nothing at all, except for one little ewe lamb. He raised it from its infancy; it grew up with his children, it shared his food, it drank from his cup, it slept in his arms, and it was regarded by him as virtually a daughter.

"One day, the rich man had a traveler come to stay at his house. Instead of sending a man out into his fields to take one of his sheep and have it killed in order that he might be able to provide for the traveler, he sent for the little ewe lamb that belonged to the poor man, and he had it killed, and that was how he provided for the traveler."

The rich man jumped up and said, "That is awful. That is totally wrong. The man who did that deserves to die for such a pitiless action."

And as those words escaped his lips, the truth suddenly occurred to him at the same moment as his friend said it out loud:

"You are that man."

The Faults of Others

What the story described, in a far less significant manner, was the circumstances of that real-life rich man who had used his power to compel a married woman to sleep with him, and who had snatched a loyal servant's wife, and had had him killed to cover it all up. That rich man was, of course, King David. The visitor was the prophet Nathan (see 2 Samuel 12). And the reason for beginning this chapter with that story is because it reveals a tendency that I find in my heart, and that perhaps you see in yours—namely, the ability to detect very quickly the failing of someone else while ignoring the failings within myself. Each of us, if we're honest, is by nature inclined to discover and condemn the faults of others while passing much more lightly over our own sins. It is this tendency that Jesus highlights as he continues this Sermon on the Plain.

In the previous chapter, we built towards Jesus' great statement about God's nature, and how we are to imitate him as his children: "Be merciful, even as your Father is merciful" (v 36). That was his summary of all that he had said concerning loving your enemies and doing good to those from whom you expect nothing in return. And what follows verse 36 is a continuation of how we will view others and treat others if our priority is to show them the kind of mercy that our heavenly Father has lavished upon us. Jesus is going to continue to call us to be very different from our natural, sinful selves, by calling us to be more and more like God himself.

What does mercy look like, then? Jesus gives us two negative commands and two positive ones:

> *"Judge not, and you will not be judged; condemn not, and you will not be condemned; forgive, and you will be forgiven; give, and it will be given to you." (Luke 6:37-38)*

Do not judge. Do not condemn. Do forgive. Do give.

This sounds simple, but it is not—for, along with the Golden Rule, the command "Judge not" is surrounded by more confusion than virtually any other verse of Scripture. You will hear the phrase "Do not judge" trotted out by the most unlikely people at the most unlikely times and used in the most unlikely ways. So, again, we need to understand exactly what Jesus is, and is not, saying here.

What "Judge Not" Does Not Mean

First of all, Jesus does *not* mean that the exercise of justice in a court of law is prohibited. Some thinkers, among them the great Russian novelist Leo Tolstoy, have taken this phrase to mean that we must set aside human law courts. But if (as we should) we allow the Bible to interpret the Bible, it is clear that this cannot be what Jesus is saying. Rulers uphold justice because a ruler is "God's servant for your good ... an avenger who carries out God's wrath on the wrongdoer" (Romans 13:4). "An eye for an eye, and a tooth for a tooth" is a principle of justice belonging to the law courts, and Jesus is not prohibiting the administration of justice here. He is talking about individual relationships, not systems of human justice.

Second, he is *not* calling for us to suspend our critical faculties. We tend to think that if someone is critical, then that's a negative thing. Not so! We have to have critical faculties in order to discriminate between truth and error, between good and bad, between right and wrong. This is the way this verse is most often misunderstood, misapplied, and thrown in Christian's faces: "Jesus said not to judge others, and here you are saying this is wrong, or that is sinful." Jesus has already in his sermon used words such as "sinners," "ungrateful," and "evil." He is not telling us to set aside the use of such categories. He will go on to tell us that we can discern someone's heart by their actions— the fruit reveals the tree. Jesus' teaching requires us to use our critical faculties, not to dismiss them.

We do not have to look at evil and say, "I'm not in a position to say that this person is wrong to have done that." We do not have to live with a moral equivalence that excuses every sinful action and that never stands against injustice. Jesus is not teaching here that we are supposed to turn a blind eye to sin, that we are to refuse to point out error, or that we are to neglect to discern between good and evil.

The Spirit of Censoriousness

So, what *is* Jesus saying?! He is challenging censoriousness: a spirit of self-righteous, self-exalting, hypocritical, harsh judgmentalism. It's the kind of approach to people which seeks to avoid self-examination by highlighting and condemning the faults of others. It is negative, it is destructive, it actively seeks out the failings of others, and it is quietly delighted when it finds them. The censorious person loves to be able to find a flaw so that they can hold it up before the other person and say, "Do you see what you're like?" or so that they can hold it up in their own minds and think, "Do you see what they're like? You're better than that." It is this spirit of harsh judgmentalism that excuses our own wrongs and condemns those of others—just as David was so quick to pronounce judgment on the man who stole a sheep while the woman he had stolen from her marriage was lying in his bedroom.

John Stott sums this up helpfully:

> *"The censorious critic ... puts the worst possible construction on [other people's] motives, pours cold*

> *water on their schemes and is ungenerous towards*
> *their mistakes."* [7]

When we see it like this, it is obvious that this kind of censorious spirit completely violates the law of love, which we considered in the previous chapter.

Do you sense any of this in yourself? In the way you treat your children, or the children of others? In the way you treat your spouse? In the way you treat your employees or your boss? In the way you treat others in your church? This area is a minefield for me. I do not seek to challenge you as someone who themselves has this all sorted out, but as a fellow struggler who knows how far short of the mark he continually falls. The finger points at me on this as much as it may point at you. And so we need to head back up to Luke 6:36, and to the promise it contains: "Your Father is merciful." When I fall short, he does not. When I fail to show mercy to others, and come back to him and admit this, he does not fail to show mercy to me. And he won't fail to show it to you.

Evangelical Judgmentalism

Reformed churches—churches in which there is a strong desire to maintain theological purity, moral rectitude, and clear expectations regarding church membership—are perhaps most in danger of coming down on the wrong side of what Jesus is saying here. We are rightly nervous of ending up with a position of theological vagueness, of never taking a position or challenging anything or anyone. But Jesus is not willing for us to adopt the other extreme while

---

7 *The Message of the Sermon on the Mount: Christian Counter-Culture*, p176.

feeling good that we have our doctrine nailed down and our moral codes worked up and our church membership classes worked through, and therefore adopting a spirit of harsh judgmentalism regarding those individuals or other churches who do not "match up"—who are not, we think deep down, doing Christianity as well as we are.

All of us by character will tend towards one of those extremes or the other. If you ask a child what they would do if they were headteacher of their school, they will either gleefully tell you that they would get rid of all the rules and let everyone do what they want (that way lies chaos and misery as well as, it would seem, a lot of candy being consumed on school premises); or they would start to give out lots of imaginary detentions, enjoy making up the rules themselves, and announce fines for various infringements. The point is that for many of us, we would enjoy using a position of leadership to set up our own standards, to judge and condemn others.

But the truth is that we make awful judges of others. Why? Because we cannot read each other's hearts. We are unable to accurately assess each other's motives, and we cannot know the weight of the burdens others are carrying. Therefore, I need to be exceptionally wary in pronouncing condemnation. And I need to be exceptionally wary in what I say about others to others. We have a very clever way in evangelical circles of criticizing others or making ourselves look good by comparison, while dressing up such censoriousness as a spiritual concern or a prayer request. This is hard to notice and to root out, but a good way to start is by taking to heart the Bible's wisdom when it comes to our speech. For instance:

> "Whoever goes about slandering reveals secrets,
>   but he who is trustworthy in spirit keeps a thing
>   covered." (Proverbs 11:13)

Or…

> "Be quick to hear, slow to speak, slow to anger."
>   (James 1:19)

Then, with this kind of divine wisdom in mind, we can learn to ask ourselves, "Is it kind, is it true, is it necessary?" We'd be a lot quieter if we filtered our words through these metrics before we ever uttered them. As the poet Grace Castle said over a hundred years ago, even in an age before social media catalyzed our ability to judge at speed and speak without thinking:

> If all that we say
> In a single day,
> With never a word left out,
>   Were printed each night,
>   In clear black and white,
> It would make strange reading, no doubt.
>
> And then just suppose,
>   Ere our eyes should close,
> We must read the whole record through.
>   Then wouldn't we sigh
>   And wouldn't we try
> A great deal less talking to do?
>
>   And I more than half think
>   That many a kink
> Would be smoother in life's tangled thread

If half that I say
In a single day
Were to be left forever unsaid.[8]

If I am prepared to put myself in the other person's shoes, and if I am prepared honestly to wish for them what I wish for myself, in obedience to the Golden Rule, then I will be prepared to replace meanness with generosity, harshness with understanding, and cruelty with kindness.

This brings us through the negative statements and out to the positives. "Judge not," says Jesus. "Condemn not," says Jesus. Instead, forgive, and give.

Forgiveness Is The Way

Think for just a moment about the kind of transformation that would be brought about in our relationships if we were to take seriously this one dramatic directive: "Forgive." The word translated forgive here is *apoluo*; it actually means "release." The bondage in which individuals and families and couples and churches and groups live can often be traced to an unwillingness to obey this one simple directive: "Forgive." It's not the same as "Excuse." It's not the same as "Deny." It's not the same as "Just forget about it for a while, and it will just all pass over and be gone." It is actually an act of the will, driven by the word of God, enabled by the Spirit of God, to recognize that someone has wronged you but not to condemn them, and instead to forgive them.

Again, forgiveness is an aspect of living out the family likeness. We are to forgive because we know we are

8 Grace W. Castle, "Suppose." The Christian Century XXIX:3 (January 18, 1912), 16 (paraphrased).

forgiven. We *can* forgive because we know we are forgiven. William Shakespeare wrote in *The Merchant of Venice*:

> *"Though justice be thy plea, consider this—*
> *That in the course of justice none of us*
> *Should see salvation. We do pray for mercy,*
> *And that same prayer doth teach us all to render*
> *The deeds of mercy."*

Every time that I refuse to forgive from the very bottom of my heart, it is a cold and deliberate choice. And every time that you and I make that cold and deliberate choice, we are deciding to mete out punishment on that person. In fact, the 19th-century poet and minister George Mac-Donald went so far as to say that unforgiveness could be worse than murder, for "the latter may be an impulse in the heat of the moment, whereas the former is a cold and deliberate choice of the heart."

But when we choose not to forgive, not only are we punishing the unforgiven person, but we are entombing ourselves, for when we cling to a grudge, we live within a dungeon of our own construction; we are trapped in the bondage of our own unforgiving hearts. There is a Chinese proverb that says, "The man who opts for revenge should dig two graves, for he will go in one of them."

I don't know where in your life this hits you, but I'm sure it hits you somewhere. Most of us are holding on to a grudge, or are choosing to bring to mind past wrongs to refresh our sense of grievance, or are looking down on someone because of a past sin committed against us or someone we love. Jesus is not calling you to say the wrong did not matter. He is calling you to say that it did matter and that you are forgiving that person anyway. Here is C.S. Lewis explaining this:

> *"Forgiving does not mean excusing. Many people seem to think it does. They think that if you ask them to forgive someone who has cheated or bullied them, you are trying to make out that there was really no cheating or no bullying. [In other words, that you say, "Well, it never really happened."] But if that were so, there would be nothing to forgive. They keep on replying, "But I tell you the man broke a most solemn promise." Exactly. That is precisely what you have to forgive. (This doesn't mean you must necessarily believe his next promise; it does mean that you must make every effort to kill every trace of resentment in your own heart, every wish to humiliate or hurt him or to pay him [back])."*[9]

Incidentally, the attitude of unforgiveness is one of the consequences of our culture turning away from the idea of sin and the reality of guilt. Of course, we do not need to feel guilty for sins committed against us rather than by us. But modern society tells us that mistakes are merely experiences to be learned from, that hurting people in order to follow what we feel will make us happy is sad but necessary, and that moral guilt is an archaic and damaging notion. Our apologies have become weak, half-hearted, and blame-deflecting. ("I'm sorry that you feel upset. I was under a lot of pressure when I said that.") But if I am not guilty, I cannot ask for forgiveness; and if I do not ask someone to forgive me, then I cannot hear them tell me

---

9 *The Weight of Glory: And Other Addresses* (HarperCollins, 1980).

that I am forgiven. And so millions of people carry around a nagging sense that they cannot name and go about their lives unforgiven and unforgiving.

The British evangelist Rico Tice says that the three most important sentences in any relationship are "I'm sorry. I was wrong. Please forgive me".[10] Jesus shows us both how to ask for forgiveness and how to give it. Do you want to know how to stay in your marriage? Forgive! Of course, marriages need more than forgiveness, but they cannot survive without less. Do you want to know how to stay in your church when somebody sins against you? Forgive them—if you need to, go and speak to them and tell them how they have hurt you, but ultimately, forgive them.

Condemnation or Forgiveness—Not Both

To forgive, first you must give up a censorious attitude, for the two cannot coexist. We must choose one or the other. This is displayed starkly in Jesus' famous parable of the prodigal son (Luke 15:11-32). When, having taken his father's inheritance money and spent it, the son comes back home, his father (who represents God) comes running out to him, hugs him, and dresses him in new clothes and jewelry. Then he throws a huge party. There is no judgment and no condemnation, but only forgiveness and restoration.

Then the older brother, who has done everything right, comes in from the fields...

"What's going on in there?"

"Hey," answers his father. "Your brother came back! It's fantastic! We're having a party to celebrate."

---

10 *So This is Christmas* (The Good Book Company, 2018), p14.

"*What?!*"

"Your brother came back! Come on in!"

"Well, hang on, I haven't been thrown a party. He has been away squandering your money on prostitutes. I have been here working hard. This makes me mad. There is no way I am celebrating his return. He shouldn't be allowed back here. *Don't you remember what he did?*"

Be merciful, Jesus says, *even as your Father is merciful.*

Here is the formula that breaks the spell. God so loved us that he sent his Son to die, that whoever believes in him shall not perish, unforgiving and unforgiven, but live—live forgiven by God and forgiving of others, and live eternally. We need, and we have, a Savior whose blood cleanses us from all sin and whose Spirit then empowers us to start looking a little more like our Father—learning not to judge, choosing not to condemn, and learning how to forgive.

If we're prepared to take this seriously, it will make a dramatic impact in our lives. I don't know the details of your life, but I do know there's much in my life that these lines speak to. Years ago, I found the Spirit of God saying to me as I considered these verses, "Listen, if you want to spend your life known for one thing, from now on and for however long you are given, why not make it that you are known for forgiveness"? I've been a pastor for 47 years, and while that brings many joys and encouragements, it also makes you vulnerable to plenty of wounds, from outside and sometimes from within your church. I have prayerfully aimed to forgive swiftly and wholly—to deal with it and forgive it, and then to not bring up the wrong done with myself in my mind or with others in conversation. That has not always been easy, and sometimes it has been very hard, and I have not always forgiven as quickly as I should have done, but it has been a freeing way to proceed.

That is what Jesus is calling all of us to—to stop condemning and be known for forgiveness. How radical would that be? How many relationships would that restore? How many hearts would that free? How many people might be won to Christ and enjoy the forgiveness he offers?

Does Generosity Overflow?

In one sense, forgiveness is a subset of generosity, for generosity is giving to others beyond what they have deserved and beyond any consideration of what we may receive in return. So, Jesus says:

> *"Give, and it will be given to you. Good measure, pressed down, shaken together, running over, will be put into your lap." (Luke 6:38)*

Kingdom subjects are generous people. As we live as God's children, giving to those around us, what is the promise? "It will be given to you." We must be careful here: Jesus is not saying, *Give, because you'll get more back*, as though generosity is actually an investment you make because it will give you a good return. That would no longer be generosity to anyone other than yourself! No: Jesus is saying, *God loves to be generous, and so his children, who are the beneficiaries of his generosity, should also display that generosity.* After all, however much you give, you cannot out-give God.

Jesus uses a word picture here to describe what God is like when it comes to giving. When I was younger, I used to buy cookies (in Scotland, we called them biscuits) for my mother at the city bakeries, and they were all in display jars. I would ask the shop assistant for, say, half a pound, and they would take a bag of the right size and shovel it in. Every so often, there would be a shopkeeper who was just manifestly generous, and so once the cookies were in the bag, they would shake them a wee bit so they settled and created more space in the top, and then they would put some more in and shake them again so they settled, and by the time they finished, you had cookies spilling out of the top. It was an expression of wonderful generosity. That's the image that is used here: "A good measure, pressed down, [and] shaken together" (v 38). The picture that Jesus' first hearers would have imagined was actually of grain rather than cookies. To carry grain, people in that society would use the bottom of their tops, which hung baggy over a belt, creating a receptacle for grain to be poured into. But the person pouring the grain in Jesus' image is so determined to give that person as much as possible that they pour it in, press it down, and pour again, until it's overflowing.

This is the way God operates, says Jesus. *He gives abundantly, overflowingly, and he keeps on doing it. And that's the way I would like you as his people to operate too.*

When I was at school, there was a shop nearby owned by a man named Mr. Entwistle. At lunchtime we would go there to buy bottles of fizzy pop. It was sold in glass bottles in those days, and they had tops on them that didn't unscrew but instead needed Mr. Entwistle to take them off with an opener. So while he wasn't looking, we would shake the bottles as hard as we could and then put them on the counter so that when he opened them, the contents would go all over the place, including all over his shirt. (Before too long he became wise to this, and when we put a bottle on the counter, he'd look at it, and then, offering us the bottle-opener, say, "That looks shook to me. You open it.")

There ought to be a sense in which people look at us as people who "look shook." They should know that with just the slightest little nudge, we would overflow with generosity and forgiveness and compassion—that what is inside us is not censoriousness or criticism but a radical mercy and kindness. In other words, when life jostles you—and from time to time it will—what overflows? In a fallen world, where that tends to be censoriousness and harshness, you have a wonderful opportunity to show how different God is, by so enjoying his forgiveness and his generosity that, when you are shaken and knocked, that is what flows from you towards others—including those, especially those, who've knocked you.

A Life of Integrity

"Each tree is known by its own fruit." Luke 6:44

I still have flashbacks from time to time to being a school-boy and taking exams. I remember the moment when, once everything was ready and we were all seated, the teacher would say, "You can turn your papers over now," and having flipped mine over and read the first question, I would immediately look around to see if everyone else felt as bad about it as I did. And sometimes, as I looked with envy on those who seemed to actually have something to say by way of answer to the question, a teacher would sidle up to my side and whisper, "Never mind looking around, Begg; just concentrate on yourself."

Well, that is exactly what Jesus asks us to do as he moves into the third section of the Sermon on the Plain. He has told us that the markers of the genuine Christian life are a complete reversal of values and an exceptional kind of love; and now, Jesus goes on to say, it involves a life of integrity.

In some measure, this is an invitation to introspection. *Do not read this sermon,* Jesus is saying, *thinking of how it applies to others and their spiritual condition. Concentrate on yourself and your own spiritual condition.* Of course, that is much more uncomfortable for us to do. But Jesus is insistent. He gives us four pictures, each of which calls us to be diligent in examining ourselves.

The Blind Leading the Blind

> *"Can a blind man lead a blind man? Will they not both fall into a pit?" (Luke 6:39)*

Over the years, every now and then I've noticed a blind person wanting to cross a busy street, and I have gone over to them to offer to help them get over safely. But imagine a blind person is trying to cross a large and busy highway, and someone says they'll help them—but that that person is themselves blind, with the result that one blind person ends up trying to help another blind man attempt to avoid four lanes of traffic. This has disaster written all over it. And that is the point that Jesus is making.

Jesus' listeners did not have to navigate four-lane roads, but they were well used to traversing rugged terrain that was full of pits and potholes, some of which you could actually fall into. But regardless of which century you live in, the answers to Jesus' questions are easy. (I would have welcomed these being the first thing I read when I turned over an exam paper at school.)

Q: Can a blind man safely lead a blind man?

A: No.

Q: Is there a strong probability that sooner or later they will both fall into a pit?

A: Yes.

Jesus is pointing out both the folly of a blind man thinking that he can act as a guide and the folly of anyone following such a guide.

How does this tie in with all that Jesus has said so far in this sermon? Well, remember the context: Jesus is teaching a crowd of 1st-century Jewish people who are used to the expositions and exhortations of the Pharisees, and those Pharisees have already taken strong exception to Jesus' words and deeds. Earlier in Luke 6, in a moment of great tension in a synagogue on a Sabbath, as Jesus came across a man with a withered hand, "the Pharisees watched him, to see whether he would heal on the Sabbath, so that they might find a reason to accuse him" (v 7). These men are keeping their eyes open for anyone who deviates from the path of holiness that they have come up with, because they have advertised themselves as those who have the clearest view of how to live for God. If you want a spiritual guide, their claim goes, you will need to go find a Pharisee. And now Jesus warns his listeners about them, for when you can't see the way, can someone else who can't see it either be any sort of an adequate guide? That way lies disaster. Later in his ministry, Jesus will make the charge explicit: when his disciples tell him that he has offended the Pharisees with his teaching, he will answer, "Let them alone: they are blind guides. And if the blind lead the blind, both will fall into a pit" (Matthew 15:14).

There is no such thing as spiritual neutrality. A teacher is always teaching either truth or error—there is nothing in between. And the test of sight is not whether you are nice or compelling or popular or smart. It is whether a teacher is teaching the Bible or not. People who speak falsehood about religious or existential matters are not benign; they are dangerous. They are at their most dangerous when they stand at a pulpit. They are a blind guide, and they are leading people to fall into the same pit that they are walking towards. They are, in other words, leading people away from the kingdom and not toward it—out of blessing and not into it—and they should be avoided at all costs.

The Teacher and the Pupil

"A disciple is not above his teacher, but everyone
when he is fully trained will be like his teacher."
(Luke 6:40)

In Jesus' time, a disciple would be virtually totally dependent upon their teacher for guidance and for instruction. They would walk with their teacher, they would eat with their teacher, and often they would live with their teacher, so that as they walked and talked, they would learn from that teacher. So in the same way that a son, no matter how advanced he may become in life, is always a son to his father, so a student, no matter how he or she may excel and go beyond the instruction and academic qualifications of their initial teacher, will (or at least should) acknowledge the debt they owe to their teacher. You sometimes hear this when someone is awarded a Ph.D. or an academic prize or honor: "In accepting this," they'll say, "I want to recognize that I owe so much to my elementary-school science teacher," or whoever it is. They are acknowledging that they owe their start to that teacher, and that much of who they are now, academically speaking, is down to the way that teacher taught and guided and molded them.

Jesus is driving home the point he began with his previous picture. If you choose a blind teacher, you won't learn to see. And what was the blindness that marked the Pharisees? It was the blindness of unbelief. But perhaps most dangerous was not that they did not believe the truth but that they did not *know* that they did not believe the truth. They were self-deceived—they thought they could see when, in point of fact, they were blind. They thought they had a clear sight of how to be saved when, in reality, they were entirely in the dark. That's the worst possible teacher to have: the teacher who is completely self-deceived and so who claims with complete sincerity to be offering the opposite of what they will deliver.

So Jesus' first two word pictures are meant to cause us to stop and ask ourselves: Who do I listen to? Who is the greatest influence on how I approach my life? Who is the "teacher" to whom I look to guide me through the busy lanes of traffic that this life leads me through? Let it be someone who teaches truth about Jesus from the word of God. Otherwise, you're blindly following a blind guide.

The Speck and the Plank

"Why do you see the speck that is in your brother's eye, but do not notice the log that is in your own eye? How can you say to your brother, 'Brother, let

> *me take out the speck that is in your eye,' when*
> *you yourself do not see the log that is in your own*
> *eye? You hypocrite, first take the log out of your*
> *own eye, and then you will see clearly to take out*
> *the speck that is in your brother's eye."*
>
> *(Luke 6:41-42)*

Our tendency, as we've already seen, is to see the flaws in others rather than the failings in ourselves. We can always find ways to ignore, excuse, or explain away our own shortcomings (I was tired. I was provoked. It wasn't that bad. It was only once. Everyone does it). Jesus is saying, *Before you run around with a mobile spiritual CAT scan for everyone around you, perform it on yourself.* The test is this: are you more aware of your own failings over the past month than you are of the failings of others? When you listen to a sermon, are you quicker to see how it applies to others you know or to yourself?

A knowledge of yourself and a preparedness to front up to the realities about yourself is a nonnegotiable prerequisite to loving others and spurring them on in their Christian life. Unless I am prepared to acknowledge what the Scottish pastor Robert Murray M'Cheyne knew of himself—that "the seeds of every sin known to men dwell in my own heart"[11]—then I will treat others from the high ground of presumption rather than coming alongside them from the low place of love. This, by the way, is where church discipline begins: with ourselves. It starts with me—with me admitting that the overwhelming likelihood is that it is not my wife who needs to change but me; that

---

11 Quoted in Andrew Bonar, *Memoir and Remains of Robert Murray M'Cheyne* (Banner of Truth, 1995), p153.

it is probably not my colleagues who are the problem but me; and so on. But everything in me works against me actually adopting this attitude, because by nature I am proud and so I like to think that though I am sinful, I am also pretty good. I would far rather notice other people's mistakes than face my own.

Jesus' word picture to deal with all this is remarkable. He does not say that there is not a place for dealing with the sin of others. But he does say we need to get the order right: first your two-by-four, and then their twig. The word translated "speck" here is *karphos*, which describes small and dry foliage. It's used in Genesis 8:11 in the Greek translation of the Old Testament, the Septuagint, to describe the olive twig the dove brings back in its beak to Noah after it has found dry land. It's the kind of thing you rake up in the yard. A twig is not nothing. You don't want to get it in your eye. But then Jesus contrasts it with a *dokos*, which means a load-bearing beam in a house or other structure. A load-bearing beam needs to be substantial. In your home, there is likely nothing larger than the load-bearing beam.

And so Jesus, as he often does, makes his point with a word-picture that uses humor to make us think hard. Imagine walking around with a huge load-bearing beam sticking out of the front of your head and being entirely oblivious to the fact that it's there. And then imagine going up to someone who has a small twig in their eye and saying...

"Excuse me, there's a twig in your eye, and you really need to take it out. Do that and you'll be fine, just as I am. Here, let me take it out."

"Erm," comes the reply. "I'm not sure you can reach to take it out. In fact, could you just back up a bit?"

"Why?"

"Well, because of that thing sticking out of your own eye."

"What thing?"

"That load-bearing beam thing."

"I don't have a thing. We're not here to talk about me. We're here to talk about you and that thing in the corner of your eye."

Why is it, Jesus is asking, *that you think you can take to yourself the privilege of dealing with everybody else's spiritual condition while frankly refusing to deal with your own.* Why is it that we think that, somehow or another, we've been given the prerogative to call people up, to invite them to coffee, to send them little notes, and to admonish them "in the Lord" because of their twig when, in point of fact, we are a walking contradiction who refuses to take a proper look in the mirror?

There's a word for someone who does this, and Jesus uses it—"hypocrite" (Luke 6:42). Many people don't like churches and won't engage with the message preached by churches because, they say, "Churches are full of hypocrites. They call out everyone else and tell us we're wrong when all the time they're no better—in fact, they're worse." And they're right, and that's inexcusable. That's what Jesus is saying here. What makes this so unpleasant is that it is an apparent act of kindness. But it's not really done out of concern for the other person but rather in order to bolster our own sense of superiority. That's the hypocrisy: I feel that I can deal with sin vicariously by finding it in my brother and sister and condemning it there, without ever dealing with it here, in me, so that I can enjoy the sensation of righteousness without facing the pain of penitence.

Jesus is not at all saying that we can never show someone else their sin or warn them of their direction of travel. Specks need to be dealt with, for they stop us seeing clearly, and they cause pain. But "first take the log out of your own eye, *and then* you will see clearly to take out the speck that is in your brother's eye" (emphasis added). Deal with yourself first. Learn, says Jesus, to be as critical of yourself as you naturally are of others, and be as generous to others as you naturally are with yourself.

In other words, rigid self-examination should precede and will often preclude the kind of judgment that Jesus condemned in verse 37. Once the plank is being dealt with, and only then, and not until then, will you "see clearly [enough] to take out the speck that is in your brother's eye." Only when repentance and reformation has taken place will it be possible for us to see clearly enough to help others.

A Tree and Its Fruit

> *"For no good tree bears bad fruit, nor again does*
> *a bad tree bear good fruit, for each tree is known*
> *by its own fruit. For figs are not gathered from*
> *thornbushes, nor are grapes picked from a bramble*
> *bush. The good person out of the good treasure of*
> *his heart produces good, and the evil person out*
> *of his evil treasure produces evil, for out of the*
> *abundance of the heart his mouth speaks."*
>
> *(Luke 6:43-45)*

Thorns and briars simply do not produce figs and grapes. You can tell the identity of a tree by its fruit. If you want to know whether you have a good tree or a bad one, therefore, just look at its fruit. The point of the picture is simple: it will be the actions of a disciple that show whether he or she truly is a disciple.

So what is the "fruit" for which we should look? First, it's our character. The fruit of the Spirit is "love, joy, peace, patience, kindness, goodness, faithfulness, gentleness, self-control" (Galatians 5:22-23). So if the Spirit lives within us, these are the characteristics which will be increasingly evident in us. A religious teacher or a church pastor who is not growing in these things is likely a blind guide, whatever they say and no matter what their reputation is. A professing Christian who is not growing in these things needs to ask themselves whether they really are a disciple of Jesus, whatever their involvement in their church and no matter how often they say their prayers.

Second, our fruit is our words. "Out of the abundance of the heart [the] mouth speaks." The general tone and content of our words show what we truly are. Of course, none of us are perfect in what we say: "No human being can tame the tongue" fully and perfectly (James 3:8). But words that are angry, divisive, proud, condemnatory, and so on should be aberrations—deviations from the norm. The hallmarks of our speech, every day, in every situation, should be gentleness, generosity, humility, and kindness.

So again, Jesus is challenging us to look at ourselves. Imagine that your conversation for a day was recorded— as you talk over meals, while you grab a coffee with a colleague, when you attend a church event, as you interact with your family, everything—and then played back and analyzed. What words would describe its general content and tone? "No good tree bears bad fruit, nor again does a bad tree bear good fruit, for each tree is known by its own fruit."

And this applies to our teachers too. Of course, our pastors are not perfect; they are sheep in need of a shepherd and sinners in need of a Savior, just like every Christian. We must not hold them to a standard of perfection and condemn them when they fall short. (Jesus already spoke to us about that kind of attitude in Luke 6:41-42.) But over time, over the long haul, we must be able to say of our teachers, "Their character and the content of their speech, while not perfect, are trending in the right direction. They are honest and contrite before the Scriptures. They are kind and humble in their speech. We can see the Spirit's work in their character." No one can lead souls heavenward unless they are climbing themselves; they may have a long way to go, but they must be moving upwards.

Kingdom life involves having integrity—what we are like on the inside matching what we project on the outside and being quicker to admit our own struggles than to point out how others struggle. That requires humility, and a wise choice of who we listen to and emulate. But there is blessing in such a life. For, just as a man straddling a boat and a riverbank will never feel stable, and may find his feet moving further and further apart and making him feel more and more uncomfortable, so the person who seeks to live with one foot in and one foot out of the kingdom, or who seeks to look better to others than they really are, will find that a tense and exhausting experience. There is joy in being willing to own our sin, knowing it to be forgiven; and in being slow to speak, knowing there is wisdom in thoughtfulness; and in being quick to ask the Spirit to be at work in our hearts so that inside and then outside we are being changed more and more into the likeness of our King.

A Genuine Desire
To Obey

"Everyone who comes to me and hears my words and
does them ... is like a man building a house, who
dug deep and laid the foundation on the rock."
Luke 6:47-48

Christians are those who confess Jesus to be Lord. But, as Jesus is about to tell us, not everyone who confesses Jesus to be Lord is a Christian. The crucial question, therefore, and the one that Jesus poses as he reaches the conclusion of this most challenging of sermons, is this: does your life match your lips?

Do not move too fast past that question, nor assume that it is addressed to others but not to you. Luke told us at the very beginning of his account of Jesus' message that he was speaking to "a great crowd of his disciples and a great multitude of people from all Judea and Jerusalem and the seacoast of Tyre and Sidon (v 17). They had come "to hear him and to be healed" (v 18). In other words, Jesus was addressing a group who might loosely be described as "followers." Those listening that day were not dissimilar to those you would find in an average church on an average Sunday today: the interested, the eager, the intrigued, the expectant, the confused, the complacent, the faithful—indeed, they were not dissimilar to those who will likely pick up and read this book. You will find yourself among them, as do I.

And it is this great mix of people that Jesus wants to leave with this question: On what basis can I know that Jesus truly is my "Lord and Master"? On what basis can I know that I really am in his kingdom? He wanted them and us to be in no doubt about what it means to truly have him as our King.

Jesus has already shown us the kind of life that will be emblematic of those who can say with accuracy that they truly follow Jesus. First, it is a life that embraces a reversal of the values which are dominant in our culture, and have been in every culture through history. It is to prize what the world thinks pitiable and to question what the world deems desirable—to accept that there will be a sense of dissonance between how we and others look at the world, what we and others emphasize in life, and how we and others choose to speak. It is to be able to say, "I used to be happy to go along with this. I used to be able to speak in this way. I used to be able to laugh at these jokes. I used to be able to ignore that injustice. But now I cannot be like that—indeed, I don't want to be like that—because Jesus is Lord of my life."

Second, those who are able to justifiably declare the lordship of Jesus will also display a love that is quite exceptional: not reciprocal "love"—a kind of "I'll scratch your back if you'll scratch mine"—nor a superficial "love," the common courtesies of interaction. It is a love that is like God's; a love that is kind to the ungrateful and the wicked and a love marked by forgiveness and generosity.

Third, the life of someone whose Lord really is Jesus will be marked by an integrity that is quick to confess their own shortcomings and sins, gentle in helping others with theirs, and prepared to face up to the challenge that "out of the abundance of the heart [the] mouth speaks" (v 45).

Now, fourth, Jesus says that those who genuinely know him will make that plain through a genuine desire to obey him.

Therefore, what we do with Jesus' words is a great signpost of our true identity and our eternal destiny. Jesus stands as the fork in the road. This was what Simeon had prophetically realized as he held the infant Jesus in his arms: "This child," he told Mary and Joseph, "is appointed for the fall and rising of many in Israel, and for a sign that is opposed … so that thoughts from many hearts may be revealed" (v 34-35). This was what John the Baptist had prophetically revealed as he pointed to the one who was to follow him: "His winnowing fork is in his hand, to clear his threshing floor and to gather the wheat into his barn, but the chaff he will burn with unquenchable fire" (3:17). Those who will bow beneath his lordship, Simeon and John were saying, will be gathered in by him and will rise up into all that is prepared for his people to enjoy in eternity. Those who will refuse to bow beneath his lordship, though, will fall, will be cast out, and will spend eternity without him.

There can, therefore, be no more important question than that of what we do with Jesus. And so we return to the question on which hangs eternity: do we truly have Jesus as our Lord?

Orthodox, Enthusiastic, and Not Actually Christian

As if to shake us out of any complacency that remains as he approaches the end of his sermon, Jesus asks a simple question: "Why do you call me 'Lord, Lord,' and not do what I tell you?" (6:46). These words contain a warning, conduct an investigation, and demand some self-examination. Jesus is aiming at those for whom there is a great gap between their saying and their doing. He is asking whether your verbal profession is accompanied by moral obedience.

Jesus posed this challenge on more than one occasion. In Matthew 7, preaching a similar sermon, Jesus put it this way: "Not everyone," he says, "who says to me, 'Lord, Lord,' will enter the kingdom of heaven." Imagine listening to that. The natural and correct response would be to ask, "Well, who *is* going to enter the kingdom of heaven? If it's not the people who say, 'Lord, Lord,' who *is* in the kingdom?" *Well,* says Jesus, *the only people that go into heaven are the ones who do the will of my Father, who is in heaven. In fact,* he continues, *I want you to understand that on the day when I come to save and to judge, many people will say,* "Lord, Lord, did we not prophesy in your name, and cast out demons in your name, and do many mighty works in your name?" (v 22). Jesus is thinking about those who can legitimately say, "Lord, we were at the very forefront of ministry. We used our gifts to serve you. We were able to do all kinds of things in your name, Lord." His response? "Then will I declare to them, 'I never knew you; depart from me, you workers of lawlessness'" (v 23).

Gathering with his people, saying all the right words, and singing the right songs is no sure indicator of a relationship with Jesus or a guarantee of admission into heaven.

Let that sink in for a moment. These are men and women who make a clear verbal profession of faith and who are active in ministry and to whom Jesus will say, "I never knew you."

Again, we need to be clear what Jesus is not saying. He is not saying that a verbal profession of faith is unimportant. "If you confess with your mouth that Jesus is Lord and believe in your heart that God raised him from the dead, you will be saved," Paul wrote to the church in Rome (Romans 10:9). In fact, it is impossible to say, "Jesus is Lord" with any sense of reality and integrity except by the enabling of the Spirit of God (1 Corinthians 12:3). Jesus is not setting aside in any way the importance—indeed, the necessity—of making a verbal profession of our faith and trust in Jesus: of our willingness to declare with our lips that Jesus is Lord. However, what Jesus is saying is that it is distinctly possible to make a verbal profession—an orthodox, enthusiastic, public verbal profession—which is, in fact, unreal.

It is possible to be used by Jesus to build his church without genuinely being a Christian. It is possible to be gifted by Jesus with various abilities without genuinely being a Christian. It is possible to have completely orthodox theology and know your Bible very well without genuinely being a Christian. Giftedness does not equal an acceptance of Jesus' lordship, and nor does being a great preacher.

John Stott, in his masterfully concise manner, says this:

> *"What better Christian profession could be given [than this]? Here are people who call Jesus 'Lord'*

> *with courtesy, orthodoxy, and enthusiasm, in*
> *private devotion and in public ministry. What*
> *can be wrong with this? In itself nothing. And yet*
> *everything is wrong because it is talk without truth,*
> *profession without reality. It will not save them on*
> *the day of judgment."* [12]

That's why the emphasis of the Bible, both for the individual in examining their life and for anyone assessing the faithfulness and health of a ministry, is on the holiness of our lives and the obedience of our hearts. Our private behavior, as much as or more than our public profession, reveals the truth or otherwise of our claim to follow Jesus as Lord. That is, the real test—and this is deeply challenging—is that we "depart from iniquity" (2 Timothy 2:19, KJV). Not that we live a perfect life but that when we are confronted by Jesus' word calling us to stop something, or take up something, or change in some way, we say, "Yes, Lord" and—whatever the cost to us and whatever the incomprehension or worse of the world around us—we work out what obedience to him needs to look like for us and then get on with it, relying on the power of the Spirit who resides within us.

Jesus is not demanding 100% success, and there will of course be disappointments and falterings and failings along the way. We will remain a long way off what we are called to be, but we will also be an increasing distance from what we once were. In other words, others will be able to say of us, "you turned to God from idols to serve the living and true God" (1 Thessalonians 1:9). We will be

---

12 *The Message of the Sermon on the Mount: Christian Counter-Culture*, p207.

different, and it will be clear to those around us that we are different. Therefore the best person to tell you whether this should be a matter of assurance or challenge for you is probably not actually you but someone else who loves Jesus and knows you well. Wisdom often looks like inviting such a loved one or friend to tell you whether and where they can see you changing and growing.

Saying "Jesus is Lord" is necessary, but it is not sufficient, according to Jesus. It is your doing that reveals the reality.

Buildings and Boats

Now Jesus arrives at another of his most famous sayings. He changes the contrast from saying and doing to *hearing* and doing:

> *"Everyone who comes to me and hears my words and does them, I will show you what he is like: he is like a man building a house, who dug deep and laid the foundation on the rock. And when a flood arose, the stream broke against that house and could not shake it, because it had been well built. But the one who hears and does not do them is like a man who built a house on the ground without a foundation. When the stream broke against it, immediately it fell, and the ruin of that house was great."*
> *(Luke 6:47-49)*

I am no builder, but I think I am safe to say that if we were to walk down a road together and see two homes under construction which had reached the wall-building stage, and were doing a reasonable job of constructing the walls, we would not be able to see any fundamental difference between them. And, if we knew nothing at all about building, and had walked down that road two weeks before, we may have wondered why the builder of the first home seemed to spend so much time digging *into* the ground rather than building *on* the ground while the second builder was already building the walls and getting the roof in place. We may even have said to ourselves, "I must make a mental note that if ever I have a house built, I should get a quote from that second builder because he is far more efficient, will waste far less of my money, and will build me a fine house much more quickly and easily."

Maybe you would not have been so naïve as to think that. But once those two homes were finished, no one would be able to see any difference between them.

Until the storms came.

In Jesus' story, it was only when the river burst its banks and the wind beat hard against the structures that the fundamental, fatal difference between the two became apparent. One—the one whose builder "dug deep and laid the foundation on the rock"—could not be shaken. The one without a foundation "fell, and the ruin of that house was great."

This is not hard to understand. We know it from experience. Anyone who has a Lego set knows that the base matters. Anyone who has put anything into the ground knows the importance of putting it in properly, which is usually not the same is putting it in quickly or without much effort. Every now and then, after a storm has swept through northeastern Ohio, I'll drive along and see some mailboxes standing tall and others lying forlorn and flat. And my suspicion is that many of those lying down were put up quickly one Saturday afternoon, and that a conversation is going on in that house along the lines of...

"Do you not think it would have been better to have dug down a little further and maybe poured in a little concrete?"

"Well, when I put it up, it looked just as good as the neighbors' across the street did, didn't it?"

"Yes, it absolutely did. But it doesn't look as good as theirs does now that the storm has passed through, does it?"

Jesus' story is humorous, but the point is deadly serious. From the outside on a Sunday morning, professing Christians tend to look much the same as each other. They go to church, they sing the songs, they hear the sermons. It is hard to see who is building their lives on the word and is a member of the kingdom—and who is not. The question for the hearers of Jesus' sermon—including me and you—is not whether we hear it; nor is it whether we affirm it, but whether we *do* it.

How, then, do we know whether Jesus is truly our Lord? It's when the flood comes, when the torrent breaks, and when our lives are turned upside down—that's when we find out. (Indeed, this is one reason why God allows trials to come into our lives—"so that the tested genuineness of your faith ... may be found to result in praise and glory and honor," 1 Peter 1:6-7.) When the storm comes, the difference between the one who merely heard the word and the one who actually built their life on the word is revealed.

To change the analogy, imagine boats on a calm sea. There they are, sitting happily, parked up. (To be honest, I don't know any more about sailing than I do about building.) Then, all of a sudden, from nowhere a huge storm comes blowing through. Some of them are turned over, some of them are cast adrift—and some stay in place, the right way up, battered by the storm but unmoved by it. Why? Because they had dropped their anchors down, and so the boats went nowhere.

So the question is, when the storms come, and they will…

Will your anchor hold in the storms of life,
When the clouds unfold their winds of strife?
When the strong tides lift, and the cables strain,
Will your anchor drift, or firm remain?

We have an anchor that keeps the soul
Steadfast and sure while the billows roll;
Fastened to the Rock which cannot move,
Grounded firm and deep in the Savior's love! [13]

The storms of life reveal whether or not that last verse is true of us. As John Calvin put it, "True piety is not distinguished from its counterfeit till it comes to the trial."[14]

A Warning and an Invitation

Again, let's be clear what Jesus is not saying when he asks if we are those who hear and do, rather than those who merely hear. He is not saying that entry into the kingdom of heaven is by way of obedience, or that he gets us started in the Christian life by grace and then we continue in it through obedience. The only way we could take that from

---

13 Priscilla J. Owens, "We Have an Anchor" (1882).
14 *Commentary on a Harmony of the Evangelists, Matthew, Mark, and Luke*, vol. 1, p370.

this passage is to take this passage out of Luke's Gospel. Jesus did not come to preach obedience but to die to rescue us. The message of Luke's Gospel is that "the Son of Man came to seek and to save the lost" (Luke 19:10). He did "not come to call the righteous" who were good at obeying him but rather "sinners," who knew they were not good at obeying him (5:32). Salvation is by grace alone, through faith alone, plus nothing. All that we bring to Christ is the sin from which we need to be forgiven.

Still, we must not miss Jesus' challenge here in what he *is* saying, which is this: those who have truly believed the gospel will seek to obey him. It is well worth reminding ourselves of what we heard from Luther in the first chapter of this book: that "Christ is saying nothing in this sermon about how we become Christians, but only about the works and fruit that no one can do unless he is a Christian and in a state of grace." But, as Luther is also generally thought to have said, it is faith alone that saves, but the faith that saves is never alone—that is, we are saved only and completely by placing our faith in our Lord Jesus' death in our place, but faith in Jesus as our Lord will inevitably lead to obedience to his commands. To use the words of the apostle John, who was one of those listening to Jesus as he preached these words, "If we say we have fellowship with him while we walk in darkness, we lie" (1 John 1:6)—we lie to ourselves if we claim to be Christ's but follow the ways of this world, which is to fall into the trap of absorption. It is why the Bible is a dangerous book to read and church is a dangerous place to be—because we can convince ourselves that, because we have heard, we are saved.

The whole sermon is a challenge and a warning—and it is an invitation. For there is a place on which you can build your life such that no storm, during this life or at the end of this life, can destroy it. There is a way to live such that you may look at any trial and say, "You may buffet me and you may bruise me, but you will never knock me flat, for I have built my life on Christ, and you cannot take Christ from me." There is a way to live such that you can even look at death and say, "You will not keep me, for my Savior lives, and he has promised me, 'Today you will be with me in paradise'" (Luke 23:43). The person who confesses Jesus as Lord with their lips and believes his promises in their heart, and therefore seeks to obey him in their lives—that is the person who can walk confidently through the storms, singing:

> *My hope is built on nothing less*
> *Than Jesus' blood and righteousness;*
> *I dare not trust the sweetest frame,*
> *But wholly lean on Jesus' name.*
> *On Christ, the solid rock, I stand;*
> *All other ground is sinking sand.*[15]

---

15 Edward Mote, "My Hope Is Built on Nothing Less" (1834).

The Heart of
Our King

"When the Lord saw her, he had compassion on her."
Luke 7:13

The Sermon on the Plain is challenging. It is an invitation to enjoy the blessing of life in Jesus' kingdom—a description of the best life we can find—but, because that life is so countercultural and counterintuitive, it requires us to take a long, hard look at ourselves. Jesus does not compromise or negotiate. If we take his words seriously, they will change us.

I do not wish, in this final chapter, to undermine or diminish any ways that the Spirit has been at work in you as you have read, to point out ways in which you need to change in order to live all out as a disciple of Jesus, or perhaps even to show you that you need truly to put your faith in him as Lord and Savior and *become* a disciple of Jesus. But at the same time, the Scriptures are first and foremost about the glory and goodness of *Jesus* rather than about *us*. As Jesus himself has said to us, each tree is known by its own fruit, and it is what a person does that reveals the heart beneath—and therefore shows whether we can trust them, and should listen to and follow them. That is true of Jesus no less than it is of anyone else. And so in this chapter, we are going to turn from what Jesus said to what Jesus is like, for the one who calls us to follow him as Lord is the one who is himself full of compassion towards us.

The Mission Statement

In Luke's Gospel, if the Sermon on the Plain is Jesus giving us his description of life in his kingdom, his words in a synagogue in a previous chapter are Jesus giving us his mission statement for his own life:

> "As was his custom, he went to the synagogue on the Sabbath day, and he stood up to read. And the scroll of the prophet Isaiah was given to him. He unrolled the scroll and found the place where it was written,

> "'The Spirit of the Lord is upon me,
>   because he has anointed me
>   to proclaim good news to the poor.
> He has sent me to proclaim liberty to the captives
>   and recovering of sight to the blind,
>   to set at liberty those who are oppressed,
> to proclaim the year of the Lord's favor.'

> "And he rolled up the scroll and gave it back to the attendant and sat down. And the eyes of all in the synagogue were fixed on him. And he began to say to them, 'Today this Scripture has been fulfilled in your hearing.'" (Luke 4:16-21)

Jesus is saying, *I am here to announce good news, to bring freedom to those oppressed by fear and darkness and death, and to herald the dawning of the Lord's favor.* But, as striking as what Jesus did say is what he did not, for in Isaiah, there is no period after "favor"—the prophet is looking forward to the one who will come "to proclaim the year of the LORD's favor, *and the day of vengeance of our God*" (Isaiah 61:2, emphasis mine).

Why did Jesus stop before reading that part? It was not because there is not a day of vengeance at all but because that day had not—and still has not—yet arrived. Jesus was saying that his ministry was supremely one of compassion and of mercy. It is as though he is the embodiment of what Paul says in Romans 2: "God's kindness is meant to lead you to repentance" (v 4)—a repentance that results in forgiveness and eternal life in place of judgment and condemnation. Jesus *is* kindness, coming to invite people to come back under his rule and enter his kingdom—coming to die in order to open that way into his kingdom for all eternity. It is likely that none of us have fully appreciated just how kind and compassionate Jesus is, as well as just how powerful he is. But these wonderful characteristics—his compassion and his power—are made plain as Jesus finishes his Sermon on the Plain and comes across two individuals, both of them racked with sadness.

Asking Is All That Is Needed

The first of those two individuals was a Roman centurion, a man who would have faced and overcome challenges on the battlefield and a man who enjoyed a position of some prominence in his community. As would have befitted a man of his status, he had slaves within his house. Romans slaves had very few rights, but this centurion had at least one servant whom he "highly valued" (Luke 7:2). This servant was now, however, "sick and at the point of death." Somehow, this Roman soldier had "heard about Jesus." Since he had not become a centurion by being a fool, he seems to have said to himself, *Jesus is Jewish, and I am not Jewish. I have some friends who are Jewish leaders. It'd be best to ask them to go make the introductions for me.* So he "sent to him elders of the Jews, asking him to come and heal his servant" (v 3). (Notice his level of faith here.)

So the Jewish elders head off to find Jesus and ask him to help the centurion. "He is worthy to have you do this for him," they tell Jesus, "for he loves our nation, and he is the one who built us our synagogue" (v 4-5). This is what we could call the religious approach to God: *Here are the good things this person has done; therefore this person is worthy of your divine help and blessing.* Before Jesus reaches his house, though, somehow the centurion hears that the Jewish elders have made their appeal on the strength of what he has done, and he seems to be horrified. So he sends some other friends of his, and through them he makes a very different kind of plea:

> *"Lord, do not trouble yourself, for I am not worthy to have you come under my roof. Therefore I did not presume to come to you. But say the word, and let my servant be healed" (v 6-7).*

Again, notice his level of faith. He trusts not in anything

he has done but in Jesus' power to help and Jesus' willingness to help.

> "When Jesus heard these things, he marveled at him, and turning to the crowd that followed him, said, 'I tell you, not even in Israel have I found such faith.' And when those who had been sent returned to the house, they found the servant well." (v 9-10)

Faith is not coming to Jesus and telling him what we have done and what we deserve; it is coming to Jesus because we know that he is compassionate and powerful; that he is willing and he is able to do what we need. Faith is coming to him, as it were, not with full hands and on our feet but with empty hands and on our knees, confident not in who we are but in who he is. The centurion knew something that the elders did not: he knew what Jesus is like.

Imagine the conversation when those elders return to the centurion's house. *We heard your servant is better!* they say with a smile. *What we said to Jesus, about your worthiness to be helped by him, obviously worked. He was persuaded.*

No, no, it was nothing to do with what you said, responds the centurion. *I sent friends to tell Jesus not to listen to you. Jesus does not need to be persuaded to help. That's to misunderstand his character completely. He stands ready to help. He does not need convincing—just asking.*

His Heart Went Out to Her

From this interaction with a Roman centurion, Luke takes us to a scene "soon afterward" where Jesus comes across a Jewish widow. Here is another sad household, for he meets a funeral procession at the center of which is a young man's body—and he was "the only son of his mother, and she was a widow" (v 12). It is the most desperate scene imaginable—this woman has buried her husband some time previously, and now she is burying her only son. In that society, she now has no means of protection or provision; from a human perspective she faces sadness, loneliness, and the end of the family line. All her hope lies cold in the corpse of her son.

And it is this funeral procession that Jesus comes across. Strikingly, nobody asks Jesus to do something. No one seems to think, *Why don't we get Jesus involved in this?* No one is expecting anything other than a routine, albeit tragic, funeral.

But "when the Lord saw her, he had compassion on her" (v 13) The NIV translates the Greek word behind "compassion" as "his heart went out to her." He does not see her simply as a sinner, so that he says, *Well, death is a reality because of sin, and you too are a sinner, under that curse.* No, he sees her as a sufferer, so that his heart goes out to her. He sees, he cares, he feels. He is not a Savior who floats two feet above the ground of Galilee, aloof and uninvolved, but one who walks the dusty roads and gets involved in the lives of those he meets. He is the God who, in his heart, is full of compassion for those who are suffering from the brokenness of life in this world, whether it is self-inflicted or not.

But Jesus does not just have the compassion to care about her grief; he also has the power to overcome death:

> *"Then he came up and touched the bier, and the bearers stood still. And he said, 'Young man, I say*

*to you, arise.' And the dead man sat up and began
to speak, and Jesus gave him to his mother."*

(v 14-15)

Jesus does what no one else can do. He halts the tragic journey to the grave. He gives this woman back her son, her future, her hope. This is who Jesus is. He is the one who has all power and authority. And this is what makes his compassion all the more magnificent—that somebody as vast in his resources would stoop to the level of this, to some anonymous woman in her miserable circumstances on a routine day as she buries her only boy. Not because she asked but because he saw and cared. He is moved not by a request but by his own compassion.

John Calvin shows us where we are in this scene: "This young man, whom Christ raised from the dead, is an emblem of the spiritual life which he restores to us." In other words, outside the town of Nain we are seeing what Jesus is like not just for this widow and her son, but for us—what Jesus does spiritually for all his people.

In the same way that he saw this funeral scene and moved towards it, so he saw our desperate plight and came to us; he became incarnate as a human.

In the same way that he touched the place of death in the midst of the funeral procession, making himself ritually unclean, so Jesus went into death himself, tasting it for us, becoming unclean, and bearing our curse and judgment.

In the same way that he spoke words that brought the son from death to life, so "an hour is coming, and is now here, when the dead will hear the voice of the Son of God, and those who hear will live" (John 5:25).

And just as it was compassion that moved him to intervene at this funeral and reverse death, so it was compassion that brought him to the world, took him to the cross, and brought him out of the grave to offer us life with him.

Jesus hears and cares about the things that make your heart heavy and your cheeks wet. And allied to that compassion is his power, so that he is the victor over death and the one who will, in full and final form, one day raise all his people and wipe all our eyes:

> *When the blest, who sleep in Jesus, at his bidding*
> *shall arise*
> *From the silence of the grave, and from the sea,*
> *And with bodies all celestial they shall meet him in*
> *the skies,*
> *What a gath'ring and rejoicing there will be!*
> *What a gath'ring, what a gath'ring,*
> *What a gath'ring of the ransomed in the summer*
> *land of love!*
> *What a gath'ring, what a gath'ring,*
> *Of the ransomed in that happy home above!* [16]

So when Jesus challenges us not just to say, "Lord, Lord" but to mean it and to live it, it is this Jesus, full of compassion and power, who is issuing that challenge. When Jesus calls us to be different—to embrace upside-down values, to pursue a different kind of love, to be marked by integrity, and to live a life of obedience—it is *this* Jesus who is calling us. It is as we look at Jesus that we will find ourselves drawn to him, to follow and serve and obey him. And it is as we look at Jesus that we discover the greatest

---

16 Fanny Crosby (1887).

blessing of all the blessings of being in his kingdom, the greatest joy of all the joys of being part of God's people, and the only thing we truly need in order to experience life at its very best, forever—Jesus himself.

Bibliography

Andrew Bonar, *Memoir and Remains of Robert Murray M'Cheyne* (Banner of Truth, 1995)

John Calvin, *Commentary on a Harmony of the Evangelists, Matthew, Mark, and Luke*, translated William Pringle (Calvin Translation Society, 1845)

Richard Lenski, *The Interpretation of St. Luke's Gospel 1–11* (Augsburg Fortress, 2008)

C.S. Lewis, *The Weight of Glory: And Other Addresses* (HarperCollins, 1980)

Jaroslav Pelikan (ed), *Luther's Works*, volume 21 (Concordia, 1958)

John Stott, *The Message of the Sermon on the Mount: Christian Counter-Culture* in The Bible Speaks Today series (IVP Academic, 1978)

Rico Tice, *So This is Christmas* (The Good Book Company, 2018)